# CONTENTS

**September 15, 2005**

**Appendix: Answers to Post-Hearing Questions**

# CYBER SECURITY: U.S. VULNERABILITY AND PREPAREDNESS

## HEARING

BEFORE THE

## COMMITTEE ON SCIENCE
## HOUSE OF REPRESENTATIVES

ONE HUNDRED NINTH CONGRESS

FIRST SESSION

SEPTEMBER 15, 2005

**Serial No. 109–25**

Printed for the use of the Committee on Science

Available via the World Wide Web: http://www.house.gov/science

U.S. GOVERNMENT PRINTING OFFICE

23–332PS WASHINGTON : 2006

For sale by the Superintendent of Documents, U.S. Government Printing Office
Internet: bookstore.gpo.gov Phone: toll free (866) 512–1800; DC area (202) 512–1800
Fax: (202) 512–2250 Mail: Stop SSOP, Washington, DC 20402–0001

# CYBER SECURITY: U.S. VULNERABILITY AND PREPAREDNESS

---

**THURSDAY, SEPTEMBER 15, 2005**

HOUSE OF REPRESENTATIVES,
COMMITTEE ON SCIENCE,
*Washington, DC.*

The Committee met, pursuant to call, at 10:00 a.m., in Room 2318 of the Rayburn House Office Building, Hon. Sherwood L. Boehlert [Chairman of the Committee] presiding.

# COMMITTEE ON SCIENCE
# U.S. HOUSE OF REPRESENTATIVES

## *Cyber Security: U.S. Vulnerability and Preparedness*

Thursday, September 15, 2005
10:00 a.m. – 12:00 p.m.
2318 Rayburn House Office Building (WEBCAST)

**Witness List**

**Mr. Donald "Andy" Purdy**
Acting Director
National Cyber Security Division
Department of Homeland Security

**Mr. John Leggate**
Chief Information Officer & Group Vice President
Digital & Communications Technology
BP Plc.

**Mr. David Kepler**
Corporate Vice President of Shared Services & Chief Information Officer
The Dow Chemical Company

**Mr. Gerald Freese**
Director of Enterprise Information Security
American Electric Power

**Mr. Andrew Geisse**
Chief Information Officer
SBC Services Inc.

Section 210 of the Congressional Accountability Act of 1995 applies the rights and protections covered under the Americans with Disabilities Act of 1990 to the United States Congress. Accordingly, the Committee on Science strives to accommodate/meet the needs of those requiring special assistance. If you need special accommodation, please contact the Committee on Science in advance of the scheduled event (3 days requested) at (202) 225-6371 or FAX (202) 225-0891.
Should you need Committee materials in alternative formats, please contact the Committee as noted above.

HEARING CHARTER

# COMMITTEE ON SCIENCE
# U.S. HOUSE OF REPRESENTATIVES

# Cyber Security: U.S. Vulnerability and Preparedness

THURSDAY, SEPTEMBER 15, 2005
10:00 A.M.–12:00 P.M.
2318 RAYBURN HOUSE OFFICE BUILDING

## 1. Purpose

On Thursday, September 15, 2005, the House Science Committee will hold a hearing to examine the extent of U.S. vulnerability to cyber attacks on critical infrastructure such as utility systems, and what the Federal Government and private sector are doing, and should be doing, to prevent and prepare for such attacks. The hearing will also examine what duties should be given to the new Assistant Secretary for Cyber Security and Telecommunications at the Department of Homeland Security.

## 2. Witnesses

**Mr. Donald "Andy" Purdy** is Acting Director of the National Cyber Security Division at the Department of Homeland Security (DHS). Prior to joining DHS, he served as senior advisor for Information Technology Security and Privacy to the President's Critical Infrastructure Protection Board.

**Mr. John Leggate** is the Chief Information Officer at BP Inc. (formerly known as British Petroleum). In addition, he is Chairman of the Chief Executive Officers' Roundtable on Digital and Cyber Infrastructure Security at the industry organization Business Executives for National Security.

**Mr. David Kepler** is Corporate Vice President of Shared Services and Chief Information Officer of The Dow Chemical Company. In addition, he leads the Chemical Sector Cyber Security Information Sharing Forum, an industry association.

**Mr. Gerald Freese** is the Director of Enterprise Information Security at American Electric Power, one of the largest electric utilities in the United States. He has also been active in the North American Electric Reliability Council-coordinated development of cyber security standards for the energy industry.

**Mr. Andrew Geisse** is the Chief Information Officer of SBC Services Inc. (formerly Southwestern Bell Corporation), the largest telecommunications carrier in the United States.

## 3. Overarching Questions

- How do critical infrastructure sectors depend on public and private information systems? What are the possible consequences for these sectors of disruption or attack on their information systems? What steps are being and should be taken to secure these systems?
- What are the most critical responsibilities of the Department of Homeland Security (DHS) in cyber security for critical infrastructure sectors, and what are the most urgent steps the new Assistant Secretary for Cyber Security and Telecommunications should take?
- In what areas are current cyber security technical solutions for critical infrastructure sectors inadequate? Where is further research needed to mitigate existing and emerging threats and vulnerabilities? How should federal agencies, such as DHS, the National Science Foundation (NSF), the National Institute of Standards and Technology (NIST), and the Defense Advanced Research Projects Agency (DARPA), and academic researchers work with industry to define priorities and support research in these areas?

**4. Issues**

**Is the U.S. adequately protecting critical information systems and is the U.S. able to detect, respond to, and recover from a cyber attacks on critical infrastructure?**

While industry and the Federal Government have increased their focus on cyber security in recent years, vulnerabilities remain, and many experts believe the U.S. needs to do more. An informal survey by a business group early this year found that in the telecommunications, energy, chemical, and transportations industries, executives estimated that 20 to 35 percent of their revenue depends directly on the Internet. Yet despite the crucial role of information technology, the vulnerabilities in information technology systems are myriad . About 10 new entries are added each day to the National Vulnerability Database (maintained by the National Institute of Standards and Technology), which contains about 12,000 entries describing vulnerabilities in commonly used information technology products. (Statistics about attacks on critical infrastructure are hard to obtain because such attacks are often not reported.)

**Is there are clear line of responsibility within the Federal Government to deal with cyber security?**

When DHS was formed in 2002, cyber security responsibilities (other than research and development) were assigned to the Assistant Secretary for Infrastructure Protection. Ever since, industry representatives have repeatedly expressed concern that cyber security has been a distant second to physical security in DHS's critical infrastructure protection activities and that the lack of a high-level official dedicated to cyber security has meant that the Department has failed to devote attention and resources to cyber security. In May 2005, the Government Accountability Office (GAO) found that DHS was having trouble with a number of its cyber responsibilities, including developing national cyber threat and vulnerability assessments and government/industry contingency recovery plans for cyber security, establishing effective partnerships with stakeholders, and achieving two-way information sharing with these stakeholders. (The summary of this report is included in Attachment A.) In response to Congressional and industry concerns, the Secretary of Homeland Security created in July the new position of Assistant Secretary for Cyber Security and Telecommunications to bring a higher profile to this area and high level attention to these problems. The position has not yet been filled.

**Are private companies doing enough to secure their information systems? To what extent are they coordinating with each other and the Federal Government on cyber security?**

The record is mixed. For many companies, it can be difficult to quantify the risks associated with their dependence on information systems and hence difficult to justify investment in cyber security. In other cases, the relevant cyber security technologies may not be available. In many industries, companies have undertaken cyber security activities within industry organizations to set standards, share best practices, and work with information technology companies to improve the security of information systems and increase their cyber security options. (The companies testifying have generally been leaders in taking cyber security seriously.) In some cases, cyber security work has been hampered by the problems in the Federal Government described above. Industry groups have indicated that they do not yet trust the processes for sharing sensitive information related to their cyber security with the government and have not yet been convinced of the value of information and services DHS would provide in return.

**What should the priorities be for federal cyber security research and development programs? Is funding for these programs adequate?**

Recommended areas for federal cyber security research in general were outlined in the recent report[1] of the President's Information Technology Advisory Committee (PITAC) and include monitoring and detection technologies, software quality assurance processes, authentication techniques, mitigation and recovery technologies, and metrics, benchmarks, and best practices. The PITAC report recommended substantial increases in funding at the National Science Foundation (NSF), DHS, and the Defense Advanced Research Projects Agency (DARPA). (Currently, funding for cyber security research programs at NSF and the National Institute of Standards and

[1] The President's Information Technology Advisory Committee released their report, *Cyber Security: A Crisis of Prioritization,* on March 18, 2005. It is available on line at *http://www.nitrd.gov/pitac/reports/20050301_cybersecurity/cybersecurity.pdf.*

Technology (NIST) is well below the levels authorized in the *Cyber Security Research and Development Act.*) The Cyber Security Industry Alliance, an association of cyber security software, hardware and services companies, the Internet Security Alliance, an association of information security users from sectors such as banking, insurance, and manufacturing, and the Information Technology Association of America, a trade association of the information technology industry, have all also publicly recommended increased federal funding for cyber security research and development.

**5. Brief Overview**

- Critical infrastructure[2] sectors include electric power generation and transmission, oil and gas production and distribution, communications, chemicals, food production, banking and finance, transportation systems, and water processing systems. These sectors are increasingly dependent on information systems to administer business operations (such as billing and supply chain management) and to monitor and control physical operations (such as manufacturing processes and distribution systems).
- As reliance on information technology grows, the number of ways that critical infrastructure systems can be interfered with and the extent of disruption or damage that can be created via such interference is also growing. In addition, the potential impact of a combined physical and cyber attack on a critical facility—e.g., using disruption of information systems to interfere with response and recovery after an explosion—would be severe.
- Some cyber security products and techniques (such as firewalls, intrusion detection systems, and virus-protection checks) can be used to safeguard many types of standard information systems (e.g., protecting billing systems and customer databases). However, specialized information technology products are often used to manage and control critical infrastructure facilities. These process control systems often use customized or older hardware and software and have different performance requirements and hence may require specialized security solutions and strategies.
- In May 2005, GAO assessed the DHS role in cyber critical infrastructure protection and found that DHS was having trouble with a number of its cyber responsibilities, including developing national cyber threat and vulnerability assessments and government/industry contingency recovery plans for cyber security (including a plan for recovering key Internet functions), establishing effective partnerships with stakeholders, and achieving two-way information sharing with these stakeholders.
- In response to stakeholder and Congressional concerns that DHS needed to make information security, particularly information security for critical infrastructure sectors, a higher priority, the Secretary of Homeland Security announced in July 2005 that the Department would create a new position of Assistant Secretary for Cyber Security and Telecommunications. This new position will have responsibility for identifying and assessing the vulnerability of critical telecommunications infrastructure and assets, providing timely and usable threat information, and leading the national response to cyber and telecommunications attacks.
- In information technology systems, new vulnerabilities and new threats emerge regularly and spread quickly. Cyber security research programs supported by the Federal Government and the private sector develop tools that provide security in the current environment, as well as produce the defenses against the next generation of cyber security risks. Following passage of the *Cyber Security Research and Development Act* in 2002, funding for National Science Foundation programs in this area has increased; however, at the same time the Defense Advanced Research Projects Agency funding for unclassified research in cyber security has dropped significantly. Other federal cyber security research and development programs exist, particularly at DHS and at the National Institute of Standards and Technology, but these are relatively small.

---

[2] As defined in the *USA PATRIOT Act* (P.L. 107–56), critical infrastructure is "systems and assets, whether physical or virtual, so vital to the United States that the incapacity or destruction of such systems and assets would have a debilitating impact on security, national economic security, national public health and safety, or any combination of those matters." This definition is used broadly throughout the Federal Government.

**6. Background**

*Critical Infrastructure Sectors and Information Security*

Critical infrastructure, as defined in the *USA PATRIOT Act*, is "systems and assets, whether physical or virtual, so vital to the United States that the incapacity or destruction of such systems and assets would have a debilitating impact on security, national economic security, national public health and safety, or any combination of those matters." Examples of critical infrastructure include electric power generation and transmission, oil and gas production and distribution, communications, chemicals, agriculture and food processing, banking and finance, transportation systems, and water processing systems. Because of its vital role in the U.S. security, economy, and quality of life, the elements of the U.S. critical infrastructure are a potential target for terrorists, who could use physical or cyber attacks to interfere with, disrupt, damage, or destroy important facilities and capabilities.

Industry is increasingly dependent on information technology for both business operations and process controls, and many of these information systems directly use, or are accessible through, public systems (e.g., the Internet) and technologies (e.g., Wi-Fi and common operating systems). Yet the Internet was not designed with security in mind.

Control systems (systems that run manufacturing and distribution facilities) raise different security issues than do the business/administrative systems. It is harder to shut the control systems down to make changes in software or hardware because doing so means shutting down an industrial operation, such as chemical manufacturing or electricity generation. In addition, the control systems operate equipment that represents a major capital expense and that is replaced or upgraded less frequently than are business systems. As a result, security fixes to control systems often require retrofitting, rather than just waiting for equipment to be replaced. Finally, while business systems (for activities like billing) are relatively similar across industries, the control systems generally use specialized protocols and configurations specific to a particular industry. As a result, customized security solutions and strategies, including specialized testing, need to be developed.

Industry responses to cyber vulnerability has depended on: (1) the type of information systems used in the sector, (2) how clear the risks associated with cyber attacks are, (3) what the value and return on investment in cyber security would be, (4) the availability of relevant cyber security technologies, and (5) (sometimes) what governmental action has been taken or is perceived as having the potential to be taken. For example, the financial and banking industries were very aggressive in adopting information security technologies, due in part to the fact that technologies to protect information and communications (the primary need in this area) have been a focus of cyber security development efforts for a long time because the extent of the vulnerability was very clear.

In other industries, there are a variety of cyber security-focused activities underway. In the electric power industry, the North American Electric Reliability Council (an industry coordination group) recently developed and adopted an interim cyber security standard that outlines minimum requirements needed to ensure the security of electronic exchange of information needed to support grid reliability and market operations; work on a permanent standard is underway. In addition, Congress has focused attention on cyber security as a key element of ensuring electric reliability and drinking water safety. The Environmental Protection Agency has worked with the industry on understanding how their water processing facilities depend on information systems and what risks that creates.

The chemical sector has developed a Chemical Sector Cyber Security Program, which is building on existing cooperative industry groups to carry out cyber security-specific activities. A sector-wide cyber security strategy was organized in 2002, and activities currently underway include work on establishing management practices, guidelines, and standards, on information sharing, and on encouraging accelerated development of improved security technologies. In addition, the chemical sector companies involved with the program support legislation that will establish national security guidelines for chemical facilities, require companies to conduct site vulnerability assessments and implement security plans, and create strong enforcement authority to help ensure facilities and systems are secure.

In addition to specific cyber security activities, all critical infrastructure sectors have Information Sharing and Analysis Centers (ISACs), which provide a forum for companies to exchange, analyze and disseminate information about vulnerabilities, threats, and incidents in a trusted environment. (The establishment of ISACs was mainly a response to Presidential Decision Directive 63 (issued in 1998), which encouraged industry to form such groups. Each ISAC has a different structure and relationship with the government, depending on the specific industry's needs, history, and regulatory environment.) In general, discussion of cyber security issues are considered an important element of ISAC-based interactions, and cross-sector discussions of cyber security issues are coordinated by the information technology sector's ISAC.

*Department of Homeland Security Cyber Security Activities and Responsibilities*

Cyber security activities at DHS are carried out in two directorates: the National Cyber Security Division (NCSD), located in the Information Analysis and Infrastructure Protection Directorate, is responsible for operational cyber security; and the Science and Technology Directorate is responsible for cyber security research and development programs.

*Operational Cyber Security at DHS*

After the recently completed department-wide Second Stage Review, the Secretary of Homeland Security has proposed and begun to implement a number of organizational changes, including the creation of an Assistant Secretary for Cyber Security and Telecommunications position. This office will be responsible for identifying and assessing the vulnerability of critical telecommunications infrastructure and assets, providing timely and usable threat information, and leading the national response to cyber and telecommunications attacks. (To date, the NCSD has reported to the existing Assistant Secretary for Infrastructure Protection; going forward, the new Assistant Secretary will be parallel to this position.[3])

The responsibilities of the NCSD are defined by several documents, including the National Strategy to Secure Cyberspace, Homeland Security Presidential Directive 7 (HSPD–7) on Critical Infrastructure Identification, Prioritization, and Protection,[4] the Interim National Infrastructure Protection Plan, and the National Response Plan. In FY06, $73 million was requested for NCSD, a $6 million increase from the level appropriated for FY05. The NCSD's mission, as defined in HSPD–7, includes analysis, warning, information sharing, vulnerability reduction, mitigation, and aiding national recovery efforts for critical infrastructure information systems.[5] Currently, within these broad goals, three areas of particular concern and focus for NCSD in the area of critical infrastructure protection are (1) strategies to improve the resiliency of the Internet against disruption, (2) improving the security of control systems, and (3) improving software assurance (trying to move from patch management to systems that emphasize security as software is being developed).

One of the most important activities of NCSD is coordination with the private sector on efforts to reduce vulnerabilities and minimize the severity of cyber attacks. Information sharing is necessary to ensure awareness of vulnerabilities, and ways to mitigate vulnerabilities, awareness of threats and attack methods, and preparedness for response and recovery. Companies are expected to be a source of information about what problems they are experiencing and what solutions have been effective, while the government (primarily via DHS) is expected to be a source of information about threats. Both government and industry acknowledge that information sharing needs to be improved. Industry has been reluctant to share sensitive information incidents. In addition, it has been unclear whether DHS has developed the policies or attracted the expertise to ensure the confidentiality of sensitive information and to provide reliable analysis and feedback about threats and potential solutions.

A variety of activities are underway in the NCSD to carry out its mission. These include the U.S. Computer Emergency Readiness Team (US–CERT), which was established in 2003 as a partnership between DHS and the public and private sectors. US–CERT is responsible for analyzing and reducing cyber threats and vulnerabilities, disseminating cyber threat warning information, and coordinating

---

[3] The new Assistant Secretary for Cyber Security and Telecommunications will be Presidentially appointed, but not Senate confirmed. The new position was announced on July 13, 2005, but as of the date of this hearing an appointment had not yet been made.

[4] Homeland Security Presidential Directive 7 (HSPD–7) on Critical Infrastructure Identification, Prioritization, and Protection is available on line at *http://www.whitehouse.gov/news/releases/2003/12/20031217-5.html.*

[5] To meet its responsibilities from HSPD–7, as well as other national strategies and plans, NCSD has defined for itself six core goals: (1) establish a National Cyber Security Response System to prevent, detect, respond to, and reconstitute rapidly after cyber incidents; (2) work with public and private sectors to reduce vulnerabilities and minimize the severity of cyber attacks; (3) promote a comprehensive national awareness program to empower American businesses, the general workforce, and the general population to secure their own parts of cyberspace; (4) foster adequate training and education programs to support the Nation's cyber security needs; (5) coordinate with the intelligence and law enforcement communities to identify and reduce threats to cyberspace; and (6) build a world-class organization that aggressively advances its cyber security mission and goals in partnership with its public and private stakeholders.

incident response activities. Another key NCSD activity is organizing exercises to test preparedness and response plans for cyber attack. The next such exercise is scheduled for November 2005 and will include public and private sector participants, including companies from the energy, financial, and transportation sectors.

*Cyber Security Research and Development at DHS*

Research and development related to cyber security are the responsibility of the DHS Science and Technology Directorate. In FY06, $16.7 million was requested for the cyber security programs in the Science and Technology Directorate, a $1.3 million decrease from the level appropriated for FY05. Specific programs focus on improving the security of Internet communication protocols and developing technologies to enhance the cyber security of critical infrastructure sectors, including of process control systems. Support and coordination is also provided for the collection of large-scale data sets about network behavior that researchers can use to better understand problems with networks and design potential solutions. Testbeds are also a critical element of DHS Science and Technology Directorate cyber security programs. They provide support for and participate in the NSF-funded Defense Technology Experimental Research (DETER) testbed (described below). They also work with the Department of Energy (at Sandia and Idaho National Laboratories) to support a control systems testbed, which is critical for design and verification of security technologies for control system applications. Since these systems often operate with real-time consequences and continuously or almost continuously, any security solution must be designed for the configuration in which the equipment and software is used and rigorously tested in realistic situations.

*Cyber Security at Other Government Agencies and Interagency Coordination*

*Operational Cyber Security*

Each critical infrastructure sector is associated with a lead government agency. For some sectors (e.g., chemicals, transportation systems, information technology and telecommunications), the lead agency is DHS, but for many other sectors, another agency is the lead (e.g., the Department of Energy for the electric power and oil and gas sectors, the Environmental Protection Agency for water treatment facilities, the Department of the Treasury for banking and finance, and the Department of Agriculture for the food sector). However, HSPD–7, the 2003 Presidential Directive that designated the lead agencies, also clearly articulated that DHS would continue to maintain an organization to serve as a focal point for the security of cyberspace. For example, DHS, the Department of Defense (DOD), and the Department of Justice co-chair the interagency National Cyber Response Coordination Group. In addition to coordinating with other agencies on the cyber security of critical infrastructure facilities, DHS also works with the Office of Management and Budget, which has significant responsibilities for the security of the Federal Government's information systems.

*Cyber Security Research and Development Programs*

Significant cyber security research and development programs are underway in a variety of federal agencies, including the National Science Foundation (NSF), the National Institute of Standards and Technology (NIST), and the Defense Advanced Research Projects Agency (DARPA). The programs at NSF and NIST were authorized by the *Cyber Security Research and Development Act* (P.L. 107–305).

At NSF, cyber security research is conducted under the auspices of the Cyber Trust program, which supports projects designed to make networked computer systems more predictable, more accountable, and less vulnerable to attack and abuse. This program is funded at $65 million in FY05, and the projects supported cover a wide variety of information security areas. Critical infrastructure applications are included; in August 2005, NSF provided funding to a new center at the University of Illinois to perform research to support the design, construction and validation of a secure cyberinfrastructure for the next-generation electric power grid. (Both the Department of Energy and DHS have pledged to collaborate with NSF to fund and manage this effort.) Another relevant project is the Cyber Defense Technology Experimental Research (DETER) testbed, which provides an experimental environment in which government, academic, and industry cyber security researchers can safely analyze and measure attacks and develop attack mitigation and confinement strategies. (DHS also provides some funding for DETER.) These research and testbeds projects also have educational elements, as the laboratories supported by those funds become centers of expertise in information systems for critical infrastructure and train the personnel that critical infrastructure companies and information technology companies need to improve the security of critical infrastructure sector applications. In addition to its cyber security research programs, NSF also supports cyber security education activities, including scholarships and curriculum development (these programs received $16 million in FY05).

At NIST, cyber security activities are centered in the Computer Security Division, which was funded at $19 million in FY05. The division's activities include developing standards, metrics, tests, guidelines, and validation programs related to information security and studying and raising awareness of information technology risks, vulnerabilities, and protection requirements. NIST also has specific responsibilities under the *Federal Information Security Management Act of 2002* for developing standards for federal information systems security and supporting federal agencies' cyber security efforts. An example of a recent NIST cyber security project (supported by DHS) is the August 2005 launch of the National Vulnerability Database, which contains about 12,000 entries describing vulnerabilities in commonly-used information technology products. (About 10 new entries are added each day.) The database integrates all publicly available U.S. Government vulnerability resources and is designed to provide references to industry resources.

A number of other agencies, mainly in DOD, have cyber security research and development activities. The DOD activities focus mainly on specific information assurance requirements related to DOD's military and intelligence missions. The Department of Energy's programs are focused primarily on applications related to the energy and electric power sectors (as in the work on control systems testbeds at Department of Energy laboratories described above).

All of these programs are coordinated through the National Science and Technology Council's (NSTC's) Interagency Working Group on Critical Information Infrastructure Protection Research and Development. In response to recommendations from the President's Information Technology Advisory Committee, this interagency group has recently been reformulated to report to both the NSTC Subcommittee on Infrastructure and its Subcommittee on Networking and Information Technology Research and Development. This group has recently begun work on defining top cyber security research and development needs and mapping those needs against current federal activities.

### 7. Witness Questions

*Questions for Mr. Andy Purdy:*

- How do critical infrastructure sectors depend on public and private information systems? What are the possible consequences for these sectors of disruption or attack on their information systems? What steps is DHS taking to help these sectors secure their systems?
- How does DHS work with the critical infrastructure sectors to gather and communicate information about threats, risks, and solutions related to cyber security?
- In what areas are current cyber security technical solutions for critical infrastructure applications inadequate? Where is further research needed to mitigate existing and emerging threats and vulnerabilities? How is DHS working with industry and academic researchers to define priorities for and support research in these areas? How does DHS coordinate these efforts within DHS and with other federal agencies, such as NSF, NIST, and DARPA?

*Questions for Mr. John Leggate:*

- How does the energy sector depend on public and private information systems? What are the possible consequences for the energy sector of disruption or attack on its information systems? What steps is BP taking to secure its systems?
- What are the most critical responsibilities of DHS in cyber security for the energy sector and what are the most urgent steps the new Assistant Secretary for Cyber Security and Telecommunications should take?
- In what areas are current cyber security technical solutions for the energy sector inadequate? Where is further research needed to mitigate existing and emerging threats and vulnerabilities? How should federal agencies, such as DHS, NSF, NIST, and DARPA, and academic researchers work with industry to define priorities for and support research in these areas?

*Questions for Mr. David Kepler:*

- How does the chemical sector depend on public and private information systems? What are the possible consequences for the chemical sector of disruption or attack on its information systems? What steps is Dow taking to secure its systems?

- What are the most critical responsibilities of DHS in cyber security for the chemical sector and what are the most urgent steps the new Assistant Secretary for Cyber Security and Telecommunications should take?
- In what areas are current cyber security technical solutions for the chemical sector inadequate? Where is further research needed to mitigate existing and emerging threats and vulnerabilities? How should federal agencies, such as DHS, NSF, NIST, and DARPA, and academic researchers work with industry to define priorities for and support research in these areas?

*Questions for Mr. Gerald Freese:*

- How does the electric power sector depend on public and private information systems? What are the possible consequences for the electric power sector of disruption or attack on its information systems? What steps is American Electric Power taking to secure its systems?
- What are the most critical responsibilities of DHS in cyber security for the electric power sector and what are the most urgent steps the new Assistant Secretary for Cyber Security and Telecommunications should take?
- In what areas are current cyber security technical solutions for the electric power sector inadequate? Where is further research needed to mitigate existing and emerging threats and vulnerabilities? How should federal agencies, such as DHS, NSF, NIST, and DARPA, and academic researchers work with industry to define priorities for and support research in these areas?

*Questions for Mr. Andrew Geisse:*

- How does the communications sector depend on public and private information systems? What are the possible consequences for the communications sector of disruption or attack on its information systems? What steps is SBC taking to secure its systems?
- What are the most critical responsibilities of DHS in cyber security for the communications sector and what are the most urgent steps the new Assistant Secretary for Cyber Security and Telecommunications should take?
- In what areas are current cyber security technical solutions for the communications sector inadequate? Where is further research needed to mitigate existing and emerging threats and vulnerabilities? How should federal agencies, such as DHS, NSF, NIST, and DARPA, and academic researchers work with industry to define priorities for and support research in these areas?

**Attachment A**

# Critical Infrastructure Protection: Department of Homeland Security Faces Challenges in Fulfilling Cyber Security Responsibilities

GOVERNMENT ACCOUNTABILITY OFFICE REPORT GAO–05–434
*http://www.gao.gov/new.items/d05434.pdf*

**Excerpt: Results in Brief**

As the focal point for critical infrastructure protection, DHS has many cyber security-related roles and responsibilities that are called for in law and policy. These responsibilities include developing plans, building partnerships, and improving information sharing, as well as implementing activities related to the five priorities in the national cyberspace strategy: (1) developing and enhancing national cyber analysis and warning, (2) reducing cyberspace threats and vulnerabilities, (3) promoting awareness of and training in security issues, (4) securing governments' cyberspace, and (5) strengthening national security and international cyberspace security cooperation. To fulfill its cyber security role, in June 2003, DHS established the National Cyber Security Division to serve as a national focal point for addressing cyber security and coordinating the implementation of cyber security efforts.

While DHS has initiated multiple efforts, it has not fully addressed any of the 13 key cyber security-related responsibilities that we identified in federal law and policy, and it has much work ahead in order to be able to fully address them. For example, DHS (1) has recently issued the Interim National Infrastructure Protection Plan, which includes cyber security elements; (2) operates the United States Computer Emergency Readiness Team to address the need for a national analysis and warning capability; and (3) has established forums to foster information sharing among federal officials with information security responsibilities and among various law enforcement entities. However, DHS has not yet developed national threat and vulnerability assessments or developed and exercised government and government/industry contingency recovery plans for cyber security, including a plan for recovering key Internet functions. Further, DHS continues to have difficulties in developing partnerships—as called for in federal policy—with other federal agencies, State and local governments, and the private sector.

DHS faces a number of challenges that have impeded its ability to fulfill its cyber CIP responsibilities. Key challenges include achieving organizational stability; gaining organizational authority; overcoming hiring and contracting issues; increasing awareness about cyber security roles and capabilities; establishing effective partnerships with stakeholders (other federal agencies, State and local governments, and the private sector); achieving two-way information sharing with these stakeholders; and demonstrating the value DHS can provide. In its strategic plan for cyber security, DHS has identified steps that can begin to address these challenges. However, until it effectively confronts and resolves these underlying challenges, DHS will have difficulty achieving significant results in strengthening the cyber security of our nation's critical infrastructures, and our nation will lack the strong cyber security focal point envisioned in federal law and policy.

We are making recommendations to the Secretary of Homeland Security to strengthen the Department's ability to implement key cyber security responsibilities by completing critical activities and resolving underlying challenges.

DHS provided written comments on a draft of this report (see app. III). In brief, DHS agreed that strengthening cyber security is central to protecting the Nation's critical infrastructures and that much remains to be done. In addition, DHS concurred with our recommendation to engage stakeholders in prioritizing its key cyber security responsibilities. However, DHS did not concur with our recommendations to identify and prioritize initiatives to address the challenges it faces, or to establish performance metrics and milestones for these initiatives. Specifically, DHS reported that its strategic plan for cyber security already provides a prioritized list, performance measures, and milestones to guide and track its activities. The department sought additional clarification of these recommendations. While we agree with DHS that its plan identifies activities (along with some performance measures and milestones) that will begin to address the challenges, this plan does not include specific initiatives that would ensure that the challenges are addressed in a prioritized and comprehensive manner. For example, the strategic plan for cyber security does not include initiatives to help stabilize and build authority for the organization. Further, the strategic plan does not identify the relative priority of its initiatives and does not consistently identify performance measures for completing its initiatives. As DHS moves forward in identifying initiatives to address the underlying challenges it faces, it will be important to establish performance measures and milestones for fulfilling these initiatives.

DHS officials (as well as others who were quoted in our report) also provided detailed technical corrections, which we have incorporated in this report as appropriate.

Chairman BOEHLERT. The Committee will come to order.

Before we proceed with today's hearing, the Committee must first dispense, very briefly, with some administrative business.

I recognize Mr. Gordon to offer a request regarding Democratic subcommittee membership.

Mr. GORDON. Thank you, Mr. Chairman.

By direction of the Democratic caucus of the Science Committee, I ask unanimous consent to ratify the election of Representative Dennis Moore of Kansas to the Subcommittee on Research, thereby filling one of the existing Democratic vacancies.

Chairman BOEHLERT. Without objection, so ordered.

That concludes the Committee's organizational business.

And we will now proceed with the hearing.

And incidentally, I can't imagine any hearing any place on this Hill, including what our colleagues in the Senate are doing with the Roberts nomination, that exceeds the importance of the topic being discussed here today. And I am so appreciative of the witnesses who have agreed to share with us and enlighten us on a very important subject matter. And I want you to know how much we welcome your appearance, because you are facilitators. We learn from you. We like to think all Members of Congress, we are all alike. We like to think we have got all of the answers. We don't even know some of the questions. But I do know this, that cyber security is critically important. And what we are about today takes us further down the path of dealing in a responsible way with this very important subject.

So I want to welcome everyone to this morning's hearing on cyber security, a subject that has long been the focus of the Science Committee.

The Nation has been making progress in developing ways to fend off and respond to cyber attacks. For example, federal agencies have been implementing our *Cyber Security Research and Development Act,* and when I say "our," I say it proudly. That is the result of this committee's work, albeit at funding levels significantly below what we would wish, and quite frankly, what is needed.

Homeland Security Secretary Michael Chertoff, responding to calls from industry and the Congress, has created the position of Assistant Secretary for Cyber Security. But as our witnesses today will make clear, we still have a very long way to go. We still pay inadequate attention to cyber security research operations in both the government and private sector. We shouldn't have to wait for the cyber equivalent of Hurricane Katrina to realize that we are inadequately prepared to prevent, detect, and respond to cyber attacks. And a cyber attack can affect a far larger area at a single stroke than can any hurricane. Not only that, given the increasing reliance of critical infrastructures on the Internet, a cyber attack could result in deaths as well as in massive, massive disruption to our economy and daily life.

There is another lesson we should take from Katrina beyond the need to prepare for real dangers that have not been recently experienced, and that is not to focus exclusively on terrorism. Cyber attacks could occur from any number of sources and motivations, even from error, not just from foreign or domestic terrorists who would do us harm.

So our goal this morning is to help develop a cyber security agenda for the Federal Government, especially to provide assistance for the new Assistant Secretary. I never want to sit on a special committee set up to investigate why we were unprepared for a cyber attack. We know we are vulnerable. It is time to act.

And I look forward to hearing from our witnesses and the guidance that they might give us to do just that.

With that, I am pleased to recognize my partner, my colleague, my friend, Mr. Gordon from Tennessee.

[The prepared statement of Chairman Boehlert follows:]

PREPARED STATEMENT OF CHAIRMAN SHERWOOD L. BOEHLERT

I want to welcome everyone to this morning's hearing on cyber security, a subject that has long been a focus of the Science Committee.

The Nation has been making progress in developing ways to fend off and respond to cyber attacks. For example, federal agencies have been implementing our *Cyber Security Research and Development Act,* albeit at funding levels significantly below what we would wish. Homeland Security Secretary Michael Chertoff, responding to calls from industry and the Congress, has created the position of Assistant Secretary for Cyber Security.

But as our witnesses today will make clear, we still have a very long way to go. We still pay inadequate attention to cyber security research and operations in both the government and private sector.

We shouldn't have to wait for the cyber equivalent of a Hurricane Katrina—or even and Hurricane Ophelia might serve—to realize that we are inadequately prepared to prevent, detect and respond to cyber attacks.

And a cyber attack can affect a far larger area at a single stroke that can any hurricane. Not only that, given the increasing reliance of critical infrastructures on the Internet, a cyber attack could result in deaths as well as in massive disruption to the economy and daily life.

There's another lesson we should take from Katrina beyond the need to prepare for real dangers that have not been recently experienced. And that is not to focus exclusively on terrorism. Cyber attacks could occur from any number of sources and motivations—even from error—not just from foreign or domestic terrorists.

So our goal this morning is to help develop a cyber security agenda for the Federal Government, especially for the new Assistant Secretary. I never want to have to sit on a special committee set up to investigate why we were unprepared for a cyber attack. We know we are vulnerable, it's time to act.

I look forward to hearing our witnesses' guidance on how to do just that.

Mr. GORDON. Thank you, Mr. Chairman.

As usual, I want to concur with your remarks, particularly in context to the urgency and the seriousness of this issue.

Today's hearing has two important purposes: to assess the progress in improving the security of computer systems on which critical industries rely, and to explore why progress has been so slow.

Networked information systems are key components of many of the Nation's critical infrastructures, including electrical power distribution, banking, finance, water supply, and telecommunications.

Computer system vulnerabilities persist worldwide, and the initiators of random cyber attacks that plague the Internet remain largely unknown.

But we know that many international terrorist groups now actively use computers and the Internet to communicate, and they are clearly capable of developing or acquiring the technical skills to direct a coordinated attack against networked computers in the United States.

The disruptions and economic damages that could result from a successful cyber attack to one or more of our critical infrastructures could be substantial. And damage to water supply systems or to the chemical processing plants, for example, could also create life-threatening consequences.

Following the events of 9/11, ensuring that security of critical infrastructure has become a national priority, but progress in securing the cyber infrastructure has simply been too slow.

A presidential directive from the Clinton Administration, PDD–63, instituted policies and established a new organization to improve the Nation's ability to detect and respond to cyber attacks, including mechanisms to improve communications between the public and the private sectors regarding cyber security matters. Subsequently, the new Department of Homeland Security was charged to be the government's focal point for cyber security.

And yet, in a report released this summer, GAO found that the Department of Homeland Security has not yet developed national cyber threat and vulnerability assessments or government/industry contingencies to recovery plans for cyber security. This is simply not good enough.

Recent events make all too clear that inadequate recovery plans, either by design or execution, have dire consequences for the citizens' health and well being. Inaction can be an enemy just as lethal as terrorists.

GAO stressed that to be successful in meeting its responsibilities, the Department will need to achieve organizational stability for cyber security activities, including the elevation of its function within the Department.

In addition, GAO indicates the Department must work to develop effective partnerships with stakeholders, and then achieve two-way information sharing with those stakeholders.

Today, we have an opportunity to hear from some of those stakeholders about what is being done within their industry sectors—to improve cyber security, where they now stand, and what could be done to accelerate progress.

I am interested in hearing about their relationship to and interactions with the Department of Homeland Security and in their views on how the government can be more effective in achieving the overall goal of cyber security for critical infrastructures.

We need to understand what the fundamental impediments are to securing cyberspace and to take appropriate action to overcome them.

And let me just conclude by saying this. As I was reviewing the briefing material for this hearing, it is inevitable that you look at it in context to Katrina. And some might say, "Well, the financial services, you know, if a bank in New Orleans or electrical power or a telecommunication outfit has several pipes that burst and they are flooded, well, you know, at least an inconvenience, but the private sector will come in and, through competition, will take care of those customers."

But what if all of the banks, what if all of the power systems go out of order? Well, it goes beyond just being a regional concern. It becomes a national concern. It means heartache and distraughtness for those individuals there, but for the American public, it means a big bill. We are spending $200 billion or more to clean up the mess from Katrina.

You know, I don't want to see, as the Chairman said, you know, I don't want to be here at a hearing later on saying, "What went wrong? And how can we improve this thing?" I mean, the fact of the matter is that when the price of gas is stable, you know, nobody is really complaining, but when it spikes up and again, this is a private sector matter—but when it spikes up, the public says, "Where are the bums in Washington? What are you doing?"

Well, you know, we want to get in front of this. And quite frankly, after four years of Homeland Security working on this problem, we are not where we need to be, and we are not where we should be. I hope that this will be an impetus today to change that and to move that forward.

And so with that, Mr. Chairman, I again join you in welcoming these witnesses. This is an important hearing, and I look forward to moving forward with it.

[The prepared statement of Mr. Gordon follows:]

PREPARED STATEMENT OF REPRESENTATIVE BART GORDON

Today's hearing has two important purposes: To assess progress in improving the security of computer systems on which critical industries rely and to explore why progress has been so slow.

Networked information systems are key components of many of the Nation's critical infrastructures, including electric power distribution, banking and finance, water supply, and telecommunications.

Computer system vulnerabilities persist worldwide, and the initiators of random cyber attacks that plague the Internet remain largely unknown.

But we know that many international terrorist groups now actively use computers and the Internet to communicate, and they are clearly capable of developing or acquiring the technical skills to direct a coordinated attack against networked computers in the United States.

The disruptions and economic damages that could result from a successful cyber attack to one or more of our critical infrastructures could be substantial. And damage to water supply systems or to chemical processing plants, for example, could also create life threatening consequences.

Following the events of 9/11, ensuring the security of critical infrastructures has become a national priority, but progress in securing the cyber infrastructure has simply been too slow.

A presidential directive from the Clinton Administration, PDD–63, instituted policies and established new organizations to improve the Nation's ability to detect and respond to cyber attacks, including mechanisms to improve communication between the public and private sectors regarding cyber security matters. Subsequently, the new Department of Homeland Security was charged to be the government's focal point for cyber security.

And yet, in a report released this summer, GAO found that the Department of Homeland Security has not yet developed national cyber threat and vulnerability assessments or government/industry contingency recovery plans for cyber security. This is simply not good enough.

Recent events make all too clear that inadequate recovery plans, either by design or execution, have dire consequences for the health and well being of our citizens. Inaction can be an enemy just as lethal as terrorists.

GAO stresses that to be successful in meeting its responsibilities, the Department will need to achieve organizational stability for cyber security activities, including an elevation of this function within the Department.

In addition, GAO indicates the Department must work to develop effective partnerships with stakeholders, and then achieve two-way information sharing with these stakeholders.

Today, we have an opportunity to hear from some of the stakeholders about what is being done within their industry sectors to improve cyber security, where they now stand, and what could be done to accelerate progress.

I am interested in hearing about their relationship to and interactions with the Department of Homeland Security and in their views on how the government can be more effective in achieving the overall goal of cyber security for critical infrastructures.

We need to understand what the fundamental impediments are to securing cyber space and to take appropriate action to overcome them.

Mr. Chairman, I want to thank you for calling this hearing, and I look forward to our discussion with the panel.

[The prepared statement of Mr. Costello follows:]

PREPARED STATEMENT OF REPRESENTATIVE JERRY F. COSTELLO

Good morning. I want to thank the witnesses for appearing before our committee to examine the current state of cyber security, how various critical infrastructure sectors depend on information systems, and what is and should be done to secure these systems. In addition, I am pleased today's hearing will also explore the respective roles of the Federal Government and private sector with respect to cyber security.

Certain socio-economic activities are vital to the day-to-day functioning and security of the country; for example, transportation of goods and people, communications, banking and finance, and the supply and distribution of electricity and water. Domestic security and our ability to monitor, deter, and respond to outside acts also depend on some of these activities as well as other more specialized activities like intelligence gathering and command and control of police and military forces. A serious disruption in these activities and capabilities could have a major impact on the country's well-being.

Even before the terrorist attacks of September 2001, concerns had been rising among security experts about the vulnerabilities to attack of computer systems and associated infrastructure. Yet, despite increasing attention from Federal and State governments and international organizations, the defense against attacks on these systems has appeared to be generally fragmented and varying widely in effectiveness. Concerns have grown that what is needed is a national cyber security framework—a coordinated, coherent set of public- and private-sector efforts required to ensure an acceptable level of cyber security for the Nation.

While industry and the Federal Government have increased their focus on cyber security in recent years, vulnerabilities remain, despite passage of the *Cyber Security Research and Development Act.* The bill authorized $903 million over five years for new federal programs to ensure that the U.S. is better prepared to prevent and combat terrorist attacks on private and government computers. The legislation was developed following a series of post-September 11, 2001 Science Committee hearings on the emerging cyber terrorist threat and the lack of a coordinated U.S. response. Despite this legislative and programmatic initiative, our computer and communications networks, upon which the country's economic and critical infrastructures for finance, transportation, energy and water distribution, and health and emergency services depend, are still among the Nation's vulnerabilities.

Valid concerns remain that the U.S. is still not appropriately organized and prepared to counter and respond to cyber security. Multiple federal agencies, as well as institutions of higher education and the private sector, have critical roles to play; yet, no enactment of or planning for the National Strategy has occurred and coordination is was lacking among agencies as they developed their research and development budget requests for FY 2006. The absence of a clear advocate for cyber security at the Department of Homeland Security, coupled with the multiple senior DHS cyber security officials leaving the department sends a clear signal to Congress that the National Cyber Security Division does not have enough authority to work effectively with the private sector. I am aware that legislation has been proposed to elevate the head of the cyber security office to the assistant secretary level to give cyber security more visibility within DHS and to allow higher level input to national policy decisions, and consider this a positive step in the right direction.

I again thank the witnesses for being with us today and providing testimony to our committee.

[The prepared statement of Ms. Johnson follows:]

PREPARED STATEMENT OF REPRESENTATIVE EDDIE BERNICE JOHNSON

Mr. Chairman and Ranking Member, I am pleased that the Science Committee is discussing our nation's cyber security today.

I appreciate each guest being here today. You all are uniquely qualified to speak about how well our infrastructure and policies are set up to handle disruptions or attacks on critical information systems.

Every year, the world relies more heavily on information technology. We view our banking accounts over the Internet, we apply for loans on-line, we even pay our bills on-line. We manage our prescriptions on-line, and there's not much today we DON'T do on-line.

We hear of small- and large-scale breaches in the security of our on-line information. One situation that comes to mind is of a large bank that had to contact all of its members because sensitive financial information had become insecure.

Congress needs to exert leadership in the area of cyber security. Our current system contains a patchwork of programs that represents neither an efficient nor effective coordinated federal effort.

I am interested to hear from today's witnesses how we can improve our current efforts in this critical area.

Thank you, Mr. Chairman. I yield back and reserve the balance of my time.

[The prepared statement of Mr. Carnahan follows:]

PREPARED STATEMENT OF REPRESENTATIVE RUSS CARNAHAN

Mr. Chairman and Mr. Ranking Member, thank you for hosting this hearing. Mr. Purdy, Mr. Leggate, Mr. Freese, Mr. Kepler, and Mr. Geisse, thank you for joining us today to discuss the future cyber security of our nation. I am very interested in how we can improve this critical infrastructure and our nation's security.

In May 2005, the GAO released a report entitled "Critical Infrastructure Protection: Challenges in Addressing Cyber Security." I hope that you will touch on some of the issues raised in this report and suggest potential options to ensure the security of our cyber infrastructure. Information sharing lapses between the public and private sectors is one of the most critical areas raised by the GAO study. It is my hope that today's hearing will help us understand opportunities for improvement.

We are pleased to have you with us and I look forward to hearing your testimony.

Chairman BOEHLERT. Thank you very much, Mr. Gordon, for those very well thought out and well reasoned arguments.

Once again, as so frequently occurs on this committee, there is not strong disagreement. There is strength in the compatibility of our views as we go forward on a very important subject.

Part of the problem is over at the Roberts hearing there are probably 200 press people. You know how this announcement of a hearing on cyber security is greeted outside the Committee room? With a muffled yawn, "Oh, what is cyber security?" This is a very important topic.

So let me, once again, express to all of you my deep and personal appreciation for your willingness to be guides for those of us sitting on this side of the witness table.

And Mr. Purdy, please relay to the Secretary our appreciation for the fact that he has announced the creation of the Assistant Secretary for Cyber Security position. I would hope that would be filled in a timely manner. I know attention is diverted in this critical period, in the aftermath of Katrina. All of the resources of the Federal Government, on the domestic side, are focused on that, understandably so. But that soon will be over. We are on the way to recovery and rebuilding one of the most important areas of the country.

Now we have got to get on with the job of cyber security. And I will say to my friends down in the Administration, particularly those who have the heavy responsibility of working for OMB, the Office of Management and Budget, that I would remind them that we passed the *Cyber Security Research and Development Act* in 2002. It wasn't yesterday. It wasn't last month. It wasn't last year. It was 2002.

But unfortunately, we don't control the purse strings. So we can determine the seriousness of the problem. We can provide direction in authorizing funds to address the problem in a comprehensive and meaningful way, but we don't control the purse strings. The appropriators, our colleagues on the Appropriations Committee, do. The people developing the budget, the people at OMB, do. And they better get a message from this hearing: this is a priority subject and it better get the priority attention it deserves, including within DHS and within the entire Executive Branch and the Legislative Branch of government.

Now with that, let me introduce our panel of very distinguished witnesses: Mr. Donald Purdy, Acting Director, National Cyber Security Division, the Department of Homeland Security; Mr. John Leggate, Chief Information Officer and Group Vice President, Digital & Communications Technology, BP; Mr. David Kepler, Corporate Vice President of Shared Services and Chief Information Officer, the Dow Chemical Company; Mr. Gerald Freese, Director of Enterprise Information Security, American Electric Power.

And for the purpose of an introduction, the Chair is pleased to recognize Mr. Akin.

Mr. AKIN. Thank you, Mr. Chairman.

And I really appreciate this opportunity to introduce a native son of the Show Me State, Andy Geisse, the Chief Information Officer of SBC. Andy grew up in my hometown in St. Louis, earned a Bachelor's degree in economics and mathematics from the University of Missouri, Columbia, and an MBA from Washington University also in St. Louis.

And he has had a long and illustrious career with SBC Communications, starting back in 1979 where he began as Assistant Manager in the comptroller's department of SBC's predecessor corporation, Southwestern Bell. He then held a variety of information technology, sales, and strategic marketing positions, including serving as the Director for Wireless Product Development for Southwestern Bell Mobile Systems, and Vice President and General Manager for Southwestern Bell Mobile Systems' Oklahoma and West Texas regions.

In 1995, he moved to Santiago, Chile, and served as Vice President and Chief Executive Officer of VTR Cellular. He later became President of the Board of STARTEL Communications, the first nationwide cellular company in Chile. SBC has interests in both companies.

In January of 1998, Andy moved to New York as President and General Manager of SBC's Cellular One upstate New York subsidiary. Later, he moved and became Vice President of Enterprise and OSS Systems for SBC and its subsidiaries located in California. In October of 1999, Andy was appointed Senior Vice President, Enterprise Software Solutions, responsible for cooperate-wide software solutions where he relocated again to San Antonio, Texas. And boy, the mileage is piling up here, Andy.

SBC Communications is an important and valued corporate citizen of St. Louis and Missouri. It has been a distinct pleasure working with the fine employees of SBC to ensure the citizens of my District receive excellent telecommunications services.

On behalf of Chairman Boehlert and other Members of this fine committee, welcome to Congress, Andy. Thank you.

Chairman BOEHLERT. Wow. That is quite an introduction. You know what I learned from that? It is an experience in upstate New York that makes you a very valued member for this panel.

Mr. AKIN. He has got something for everybody, Mr. Chairman.

Chairman BOEHLERT. Thank you very much, Mr. Akin.

And I ask unanimous consent that our colleague, Mr. Sessions of Texas, be permitted to sit in on this hearing. He is a very valuable Member of the entire Congress and one who is deeply and personally interested in the matter before the Committee. Mr. Sessions, do you have anything you would care to say?

Mr. SESSIONS. Mr. Chairman, thank you so much. It is good to be back over here. I have been gone from the Science Committee now for seven years.

Mr. Chairman, one might assume, after Mr. Akin and myself, that it is an Andy Geisse Day in Congress, but I wanted to take just a moment. He has been properly introduced by the gentleman from Missouri. Mr. Geisse and I have known each other for 22 years, during which time I have known Andy and his family. During the service that I spent some two years as Vice Chairman of the Cyberscience Research and Development Subcommittee for Homeland Security, I counted on Andy to provide information to me, background information that would help me to better serve not only this nation, but also that committee. And I am very happy that SBC has chosen to send Mr. Geisse up here. He is a dear friend, and I think he will add a lot to today's hearing.

And I want to thank you for allowing me to sit with you and the Members of this committee.

I yield back the time.

Chairman BOEHLERT. Thank you very much, Mr. Sessions. I do appreciate it.

Now to our witnesses. And the rule here is essentially the same as in most Committees. We ask that you try to summarize your opening statement in five minutes or thereabouts. And I am usually offended when I make that announcement, because we have very distinguished witnesses who have so much to offer and to ask them to capsulize their thinking in 300 seconds or less is sort of unrealistic. And so the Chair is not going to be arbitrary. You are the only—part of the only panel we will have before us today, and you all have so much value to add to our knowledge base. So I would ask that you be guided by the lights, not directed by the lights.

With that, Mr. Purdy, you are first up.

## STATEMENT OF MR. DONALD "ANDY" PURDY, JR., ACTING DIRECTOR, NATIONAL CYBER SECURITY DIVISION, DEPARTMENT OF HOMELAND SECURITY

Mr. PURDY. Good morning, Chairman Boehlert and distinguished Members of the Committee. My name is Andy Purdy. I am the Acting Director of the Department of Homeland Security's National Cyber Security Division.

I am delighted to appear before you to share the work of NCSD and those with whom we are partnering to secure our national cyberspace and critical infrastructure.

Pursuant to President Bush's Homeland Security Presidential Directive 7 (HSPD–7), our Infrastructure Protection Office developed the National Infrastructure Protection Plan (NIPP) to serve as a guide for addressing critical infrastructure and key resource protection. It sets forth a risk management framework for public and private sector stakeholders to work together to identify, prioritize, and conduct vulnerability assessments of critical assets and key resources in each sector. It also includes the identification of interdependencies of critical assets and key resources both within and across sectors as well as providing priority protective measures that owners and operators of such assets should undertake to secure them.

DHS recognizes that more than 85 percent of the critical infrastructure is owned by the private sector and that the development and enhancement of public-private partnership is paramount to securing our nation's assets.

As such, private sector-led sector coordinating councils are being established to work with their appropriate sector-specific agency via the government coordinating councils, which represent the government agencies that have a role in protecting their respective sectors.

Our Division was created in response to President Bush's National Strategy to Secure Cyberspace as a national focal point for cyber security. Given today's interconnected environment and the Department's integrated risk-based approach to critical infrastructure protection, our mission is to work collaboratively with public, private, and international entities to secure cyberspace and America's cyber assets. To meet that mission, we developed a strategic plan that is closely aligned with the Strategy, HSPD–7, the National Infrastructure Protection Plan, and the Cyber Annex to the National Response Plan.

To carry out our mission and related responsibilities, we have identified two overarching priorities: to build an effective National Cyberspace Response System, and implement a cyber risk management program for critical infrastructure protection.

A core component of our first priority is the US–CERT Operations Center that is a partnership between the Department and the public and private sectors to address cyber security issues. It provides a national coordination center that links public and private response capabilities to facilitate information sharing and coordinated response to help maintain the continuity of our nation's cyber infrastructure.

We worked with the Department of Defense and the Department of Justice to form the National Cyber Response Coordination Group that is the principle interagency mechanism to prepare for and respond to cyber incidents of national significance that was formalized in the Cyber Annex to the National Response Plan.

An important element of our response system is our ability to address the global nature of cyberspace. Implementation of our international cyber security strategy and its related outreach and collaboration objectives is well underway. Such international cooperation contributes to our overall global situation awareness and incident response capabilities in an area in which information moves at Internet speeds and traditional borders do not apply.

To advance the second priority of cyber risk management, we have incorporated a risk management approach aligned with the interim NIPP into its effort to better assess the threat and reduce the risk to our national cyberspace. Risk management includes risk assessment based on threat, vulnerabilities, and consequences as well as efforts to reduce the risk by addressing vulnerabilities before an attack occurs and mitigating and managing the consequences of a cyber attack that does occur.

Regarding reducing risk, our sector-specific responsibilities within the Department, among others, including the information technology sector, which we are the lead for, and the telecommunications sector, which our partner agency, the National Communications System, is responsible for.

The NIPP also includes a cross-sector cyber responsibility for us.

In addition to our specific responsibilities, there are three major components of our risk mitigation approach.

First, we have established the Internet Disruption Working Group with the National Communications System to address the resiliency and recovery of Internet functions in the case of a major cyber incident. The Department of Treasury and the Department of Defense are also engaged, and the working group is acting to extend the partnership to representatives in the private sector as well as international stakeholders.

Next, the interdependency between physical and cyber infrastructures is hardly more acute than in the use of control systems as integral operating components of many of our critical infrastructures.

Interestingly, these control systems are implemented with remote access, open connectivity, and connections to open networks, such as corporate intranets and the Internet. These make critical infrastructure assets more automated, more productive, more efficient, more innovative, but they also may expose many of those physical assets to physical consequences from cyber-related threats.

The third major component of our effort is the Software Assurance Program. Defects in software can be exploited to launch critical cyber attacks, and we have developed a comprehensive software assurance framework that addresses people, process, technology, and acquisition through the software development process.

I hope we have the opportunity in the questions to discuss our cyber R&D agenda and our relationship with the Science and Technology Director to fund those. We are committed to achieving success in our goals and objectives, but we cannot do it alone. We will continue to work with government and the private sector to leverage the efforts of all so we, as a Nation, are more secure in cyberspace and in our critical infrastructures.

Again, thank you for the opportunity to testify before you today, and I look forward to your questions.

[The prepared statement of Mr. Purdy follows:]

### Prepared Statement of Donald (Andy) Purdy, Jr.

Good morning Chairman Boehlert and distinguished Members of the Committee. My name is Andy Purdy, and I am the Acting Director of the Department of Homeland Security's National Cyber Security Division (NCSD). I am delighted to appear before you today to share with you the work of the NCSD and those with whom we are partnering to secure our national cyberspace and critical infrastructure. In my testimony today, I will provide an overview of NCSD, our operating mandates, our mission and goals, our priorities, and the programs in which we are engaged to meet those missions and goals.

**DHS and Critical Infrastructure Protection**

Over the course of the past several months Secretary Chertoff conducted a systematic evaluation of the Department's operations. On July 13th, Secretary Chertoff announced his six point agenda for the path ahead for the Department. As part of this agenda, the Secretary announced several Departmental organizational changes. Among these was the creation of a new Preparedness Directorate which would house a newly created office of the Assistant Secretary for Cyber Security and Telecommunications. Currently, cyber security is addressed by the NCSD, one of four divisions in the Office of Infrastructure Protection (IP), located within the Information Analysis and Infrastructure Protection Directorate.

In December 2003, President Bush issued Homeland Security Presidential Directive 7: Critical Infrastructure Identification, Prioritization, and Protection (HSPD–7), which established a national policy for federal departments and agencies to identify and prioritize United States critical infrastructure and key resources and to protect them from terrorist attacks. Among other things, HSPD–7 identified 17[1] critical infrastructure and key resource sectors and assigned responsibility for each to a Sector Specific Agency (SSA), with DHS serving as the overall program coordinator.

Additionally, HSPD–7 set forth how DHS should address critical infrastructure protection, including "summary of activities to be undertaken in order to: define and prioritize, reduce the vulnerability of, and coordinate the protection of critical infrastructure and key resources."[2]

To meet this mandate, IP developed the National Infrastructure Protection Plan (NIPP), a plan that is to serve as the guide for addressing critical infrastructure and key resource protection. It sets forth a risk management framework for public and private sector stakeholders to work together to identify, prioritize, and conduct vulnerability assessments of critical assets and key resources in each sector. It also includes the identification of interdependencies of critical assets and key resources both within and across the sectors, as well as providing priority protective measures that owners and operators of such assets should undertake to secure them. Recognizing that more that 85 percent of the critical infrastructure is owned and operated by the private sector and that the development of public-private partnership is paramount to securing our nation's assets, private sector-led Sector Coordinating Councils (SCCs) are being established to work with their appropriate SSA via Government Coordinating Councils, which represent the government agencies that have a role in protecting the respective sectors.

Currently, the office of Infrastructure Protection is finalizing the NIPP and it is expected to be released later this year. This finalized document will refine the public-private partnership model and a process for protecting our critical infrastructures from physical or cyber attack or natural disasters.

**DHS and Cyber Security**

In June 2003, in response to the President's *National Strategy to Secure Cyberspace* and HSPD–7, the Department of Homeland Security created the NCSD as a national focal point for cyber security. The national strategy established the following five national priorities for securing cyberspace:

| | |
|---|---|
| Priority I: | A National Cyberspace Security Response System |
| Priority II: | A National Cyberspace Security Threat and Vulnerability Reduction Program |
| Priority III: | A National Cyberspace Security Awareness and Training Program |
| Priority IV: | Securing Government's Cyberspace |
| Priority V: | National Security and International Cyberspace Security Cooperation |

[1] The NIPP identifies the following Critical Infrastructure Sectors and Key Resources: Food and Agriculture; Public Health and Health Care; Drinking Water and Wastewater; Energy; Banking and Finance; National Monuments and Icons; Defense Industrial Base; Information Technology; Telecommunications; Chemical; Transportation Systems; Emergency Services; Postal and Shipping; Dams; Government Facilities; Commercial Facilities; Nuclear Reactors, Materials, and Waste.

[2] Homeland Security Presidential Directive 7, December 17, 2003; *http://www.whitehouse.gov/news/releases/2003/12/20031217-5.html.*

Given today's interconnected environment and DHS's integrated risk-based approach to critical infrastructure protection, NCSD's mission is to work collaboratively with public, private, and international entities to secure cyberspace and America's cyber assets. To meet that mission, NCSD developed a Strategic Plan that establishes a set of goals with specific objectives for each goal, and milestones associated with each objective. The Strategic Plan goals, which are closely aligned with the Strategy, HSPD–7, the NIPP, and the Cyber Annex to the National Response Plan, are as follows:

1. Establish a National Cyberspace Response System to prevent, detect, respond to, and reconstitute rapidly after cyber incidents;
2. Work with public and private sector representatives to reduce vulnerabilities and minimize severity of cyber attacks;
3. Promote a comprehensive awareness plan to empower all Americans to secure their own parts of cyberspace;
4. Foster adequate training and education programs to support the Nation's cyber security needs;
5. Coordinate with the intelligence and law enforcement communities to identify and reduce threats to cyberspace; and
6. Build a world class organization that aggressively advances its cyber security mission and goals in partnership with its public and private stakeholders.

To meet these goals, NCSD is organized into four operating branches to address the various aspects of the risk management structure: (1) U.S. Computer Emergency Readiness Team (US–CERT) Operations to manage the 24–7 threat watch, warning, and response capability that can identify emerging threats and vulnerabilities and coordinate responses to major cyber incidents; (2) Strategic Initiatives Branch to manage activities to advance cyber security in critical infrastructure protection, control systems security, software development, training and education, exercises, and standards and best practices; (3) Outreach and Awareness Branch to manage outreach, cyber security awareness, and partnership efforts to disseminate information to key constituencies and build collaborative actions with key stakeholders; and (4) Law Enforcement and Intelligence Branch to coordinate and share information between these communities and NCSD's other constituents in the private sector, public sector, academia, and others, and also to coordinate interagency response and mitigation of cyber security incidents. Together, these branches make up NCSD's framework to address the cyber security challenges across our key stakeholder groups and build communications, collaboration, and awareness to further our collective capabilities to detect, recognize, attribute, respond to, mitigate, and reconstitute after cyber attacks.

**Cyber Security Priorities: Response and Risk Management**

The Strategy, HSPD–7, and the NIPP provide NCSD with a clear operating mission and national coordination responsibility. To carry out this mission and its related responsibilities, NCSD has identified two overarching priorities: to build an effective national cyberspace response system and to implement a cyber risk management program for critical infrastructure protection. Our focus on these two priorities and related programs addresses the overarching NIPP Risk Management methodology and establishes the framework for securing cyberspace today and a foundation for addressing cyber security for the future.

*Priority 1—Cyber Incident Management: A National Cyberspace Response System*

A core component of NCSD and our effort to establish a National Cyberspace Response System is the US–CERT Operations Center. US–CERT was established in September 2003 as a partnership between DHS and the public and private sectors to address cyber security issues. Building upon an initial partnership with the Computer Emergency Response Team Coordination Center (CERT/CC) in Carnegie Mellon University's Software Engineering Institute, US–CERT now provides a national coordination center that links public and private response capabilities to facilitate information sharing across all infrastructure sectors and to help protect and maintain the continuity of our nation's cyber infrastructure. The overarching approach to this task is to facilitate and implement systemic global and domestic coordination of deterrence from, preparation for, defense against, response to, and recovery from cyber incidents and attacks across the United States, as well as from the cyber consequences of physical attacks or natural disasters.

US–CERT has four major programs of activity. First, US–CERT is DHS's 24–7–365 cyber watch, warning, and incident response center, and it provides coordinated response to cyber incidents, a web portal for secure communications with private and public sector stakeholders, including critical infrastructure owners and operators, a daily report, a public website *(http://www.us-cert.gov/)*, and a National Cyber Alert System, which provides timely, actionable information to the public on both technical and non-technical bases. Second, US–CERT conducts malicious code analysis, provides malware technical support, and conducts cyber threat and vulnerability analysis. Third, US–CERT manages a situational awareness program and an Internet Health and Status service used by 50 government agency computer security incident response teams. Fourth, US–CERT manages programs for communication and collaboration among public agencies and key network defense service providers. In line with NCSD's close working relationship with NCS, US–CERT works closely with the National Coordinating Center for Telecommunications (NCC) to address and mitigate cyber threats including response and recovery. US–CERT also maintains a presence in the HSOC to ensure coordination throughout DHS.

As noted, NCSD has initiated a number of activities specifically to assist federal agencies in protecting their cyber infrastructure. NCSD established the Government Forum of Incident Response and Security Teams (GFIRST) to facilitate interagency information sharing and cooperation across federal agencies for readiness and response efforts. GFIRST is a group of technical and tactical practitioners of security response teams responsible for securing government information technology systems. The members work together to understand and handle computer security incidents and to encourage proactive and preventative security practices. The purpose of the GFIRST is to:

- Provide members with technical information, tools, methods, assistance, and guidance;
- Coordinate proactive liaison activities and analytical support;
- Further the development of quality products and services for the Federal Government;
- Share specific technical details regarding incidents within a trusted U.S. Government environment on a peer-to-peer basis; and
- Improve incident response operations.

GFIRST meets on a regular basis and held its first annual conference in April 2005 with more than 200 participants from Federal, State, and local governments. The conference was a major success for US–CERT, and GFIRST has established further lines of communications across organizations. The technical workshops and speakers stimulated many technical interchanges regarding cyber first responder activities. In another step forward, GFIRST held its first classified threat briefing with DHS Office of Information Analysis (IA), the Central Intelligence Agency, Department of Defense, and National Security Agency in June 2005.

US–CERT utilizes a secure collaboration platform, the US–CERT Portal, to support cyber information sharing and collaboration among the GFIRST community, and other cyber and critical infrastructure communities, such as the ISACs. The US–CERT Portal is being integrated into the Homeland Security Information Network (HSIN) and bridges the gap between the Government Coordinating Councils, the Sector Coordinating Councils, ISACs, and other private critical infrastructure information-sharing entities.

In addition to GFIRST, NCSD worked with the Department of Defense (DOD) and the Department of Justice (DOJ) to form the National Cyber Response Coordination Group (NCRCG) to provide a Federal Government approach to coordinated cyber incident response. NCSD created a Cyber Annex to the recently issued National Response Plan (NRP)[3] that provides a framework for responding to cyber incidents of national significance. As such, the Cyber Annex formalized the NCRCG as the principal federal interagency mechanism to coordinate preparation for, and response to, cyber incidents of national significance. The co-chairs of the NCRCG are DHS/NCSD, DOJ, and DOD. An additional 13 federal agencies with a statutory responsibility for and/or specific capability toward cyber security, including the intelligence community, comprise the membership. NCSD serves as the Executive Agent and point of contact for the NCRCG. The NCRCG has developed a concept of operations (CONOPS) for national cyber incident response that will be examined in the National Cyber Exercise, *Cyber Storm,* to be conducted by NCSD in November 2005, with public and private sector stakeholders.

The NCRCG is also reviewing capabilities of federal agencies from a cyber defense perspective to better leverage and coordinate the preparation for and response to significant cyber incidents. This effort will entail the following components:

[3] *http://www.dhs.gov/dhspublic/display?theme=15&content=4269*

- Mapping the current capabilities of government agencies related to cyber defense relative to detection and recognition of cyber activity of concern, attribution, response and mitigation, and reconstitution;
- Identifying capabilities within the government that US–CERT should leverage to maximize interagency coordination of cyber defense capabilities;
- Performing a gap analysis to identify the surge capabilities for possible leverage by, or collaboration with, the US–CERT for cyber defense issues in order to detect potentially damaging activity in cyberspace, to analyze exploits and warn potential victims, to coordinate incident responses, and to restore essential services that have been damaged; and
- Consider establishing formal resource sharing agreements with the other agencies per the cyber defense coordination needs identified through the process identified above.

An important element of a National Cyberspace Response System is our ability to address the global nature of cyberspace. Implementation of NCSD's international cyber security strategy and its related outreach and collaboration objectives is well underway, as we participate in bilateral and multilateral outreach efforts and have established cooperative programs with key allies and countries of interest. Such international cooperation contributes to our overall global situational awareness and incident response capabilities in an area in which information moves at Internet speed and traditional borders do not apply.

With our efforts, accomplishments, and on-going programs, NCSD has made significant progress in managing cyber incidents and has taken substantial strides toward building a National Cyberspace Response System. We know there is more to do, and we are enhancing and evolving our readiness and response programs to further our efforts and address this dynamic environment.

*Priority 2—Cyber Risk Management: Assessing the Threat and Reducing the Risk*

NCSD incorporated a risk management approach aligned with HSPD–7 and the resulting interim NIPP into its effort to better assess the threat and reduce the risk to our national cyberspace. Risk management includes risk assessment based on threat, vulnerabilities, and consequences, as well as efforts to reduce the risk by addressing vulnerabilities before an attack occurs, and mitigating and managing the consequences of a cyber attack that does occur. The NIPP risk management framework entails work with the intelligence community, law enforcement, and the private sector to better understand the cyber threat and a collaborative partnership between the private sector and Federal, State, and local governments looking at people, cyber, and physical assets to identify and prioritize those assets, assess vulnerabilities, and coordinate the protection of critical infrastructure and key resources.

With regard to assessing the threat, NCSD collaborates with the law enforcement and the intelligence communities in a number of ways. DHS assisted in the coordination of cyber-related issues for the "National Intelligence Estimate (NIE) of Cyber Threats to the U.S. Information Infrastructure." The resulting classified document issued in February 2004 details actors (nation states, terrorist groups, organized criminal groups, hackers, etc.), capabilities, and intent (where known). In addition, NCSD has infused cyber requirements into the Standing Information Needs (SINs) and Priority Information Needs (PINs) for the intelligence community and continues to collaborate with them through IA to characterize cyber threats for accuracy. Finally, the NCRCG includes law enforcement and intelligence agencies and has working groups addressing botnets and attribution issues.

The private sector is also a resource for threat and risk related information, and NCSD works with its industry stakeholders to gather and communicate that information. The US–CERT Internet Health Service enables US–CERT to gather information from private sector resources regarding vulnerabilities, network attacks, and malicious code activity and provide that information to federal agencies. In addition, NCSD has identified preparedness and response as a key area of joint public-private effort and is working with the critical infrastructure sectors to identify attack/threat scenarios against which proactive protective measures can be taken and response plans can be developed. And, DHS utilizes the ISACs and critical sector elements of the HSIN to obtain and share cyber security information.

With regard to reducing the risk, DHS's SSA responsibilities under the NIPP include the Information Technology (IT) Sector and the Telecommunications Sector. Specifically, NCSD coordinates the IT Sector, and the National Communications System (NCS), another of the divisions in the IP directorate, coordinates the Telecommunications Sector. Reflecting the increasing convergence between these two communications sectors in today's market, NCSD and NCS work together closely to coordinate all efforts to protect the Nation's critical cyber systems and the telecommunications transport layer.

The NIPP includes a cross-sector cyber responsibility for NCSD in addition to its IT Sector responsibility. The cross-sector responsibility is the collaborative effort between DHS/NCSD and the SSAs to ensure that deployed cyber elements have been secured in an appropriate and consistent manner across sectors. NCSD is responsible for providing cyber guidance to all sectors assisting them in understanding and mitigating cyber risk (including cyber infrastructure vulnerabilities) and in developing effective and appropriate protective measures. This guidance includes contributing cyber elements to the NIPP, reviewing the cyber aspects of the respective Sector Specific Plans (SSPs), and delivering cyber Critical Infrastructure Protection (CIP) training to SSAs to help them enhance the cyber aspects of their SSPs.

To implement these two NIPP Cyber elements, NCSD works with the Information Technology Information Sharing and Analysis Center (IT–ISAC) and the newly established Information Technology Sector Coordination Council (IT–SCC), as well as with the SSAs, ISACs and emerging SCCs in the other sectors.

In addition to NCSD's specific NIPP responsibilities, there are three major components to our cyber risk mitigation approach: the Internet Disruption Working Group (IDWG), the Control Systems Security Program, and the Software Assurance Program.

Protection of critical cyber assets goes hand-in-hand with protection of critical telecommunications assets; accordingly, NCSD and NCS are working closely together to collaborate on issues related to threats, identification of critical cyber assets, vulnerability and risk assessments, and development of appropriate protective measures that could be recommended for implementation by owners/operators. Within the NIPP framework, NCSD and NCS established the Internet Disruption Working Group (IDWG) in December 2004 to address the resiliency and recovery of Internet functions in case of a major cyber incident. The Department of Treasury and the Department of Defense are also engaged, and the working group is acting to extend the partnership to representatives from the private sector as well as international stakeholders. The IDWG reflects the convergence of telecommunications and information technology sectors in today's environment and the emergence of Next Generation Networks (NGN) that will compose the Internet of the future. An initial focus of the working group is to identify near-term actions related to situational awareness, protection, and response that government and its stakeholders can take to better prepare for, protect against, and mitigate nationally significant Internet disruptions.

The interdependency between physical and cyber infrastructures is hardly more acute than in the use of control systems as integral operating components by many of our critical infrastructures. "Control Systems" is a generic term applied to hardware, firmware, communications, and software used to perform vital monitoring and controlling functions of sensitive processes and enable automation of physical systems. Specific control systems used in the various critical infrastructure sectors include Supervisory Control and Data Acquisition (SCADA) systems, Process Control Systems (PCS), and Distributed Control Systems (DCS).

Examples of the critical infrastructure processes and functions that control systems monitor and control include energy transmission and distribution, pipelines, water and pumping stations, telecommunications, chemical processing, pharmaceutical production, rail and light rail, manufacturing, and food production. Increasingly, these control systems are implemented with remote access, open connectivity, and connections to open networks such as corporate intranets and the Internet. These sophisticated information technology tools are making our critical infrastructure assets more automated, more productive, more efficient, and more innovative, but they also may expose many of those physical assets to physical consequences from new, cyber-related threats and vulnerabilities.

To assure immediate attention is directed to protect these systems, NCSD established the Control Systems Security Program to coordinate efforts among Federal, State, and local governments, as well as control system owners, operators, and vendors to improve control system security within and across all critical infrastructure sectors. As part of this Program, NCSD developed a Control Systems Strategy that incorporates five highly integrated goals to address the issues and challenges associated with control systems security. As such, our control systems activities support NCSD's overall efforts to address cyber security across critical infrastructure sectors over the long-term, as well as the US–CERT's capability in the management, response, and handling of incidents, vulnerabilities, and mitigation of threat actions specific to critical control systems functions. NCSD also recognizes the significant attention being paid to PCS and SCADA security by various industry organizations in developing encryption standards, cryptography, modeling, and other tools to improve cyber security of control systems.

NCSD also established the US–CERT Control Systems Security Center (CSSC) in partnership with Idaho National Laboratory (INL) and other Department of Energy National Laboratories[4] in June 2004. The CSSC is involving other partners from control systems industry associations, universities, control systems vendors, and industry experts. Since its establishment, the CSSC has made considerable progress and some of its major accomplishments include:

- Established the US–CERT CSSC assessment and incident response facility located at INL and a US–CERT Support Operations Center for Control Systems;
- Established relationships with more than 25 potential industry partners and completed several agreements that established initial assessment, analysis, and vulnerability reduction plans within various industry sectors;
- Created the Critical Infrastructure Cyber Consequence Matrix to determine the industries of most concern, and a list of specific sites from the National Asset Database where Control Systems could cause a negative consequence due to failure or attack;
- Created a quantitative control systems cyber risk/decision analysis measurement methodology; and,
- Established the Process Control System Forum (PCSF) (in partnership with DHS's Science and Technology Directorate) with industry, academia, and government to accelerate the development of technology that will enhance the security, safety, and reliability of Control Systems, including legacy installations.

At the same time that the telecommunications and financial sectors have increased their dependence on information systems overall for information flows, service provision, and financial transactions, the energy, chemical, nuclear, food and agriculture, transportation, and water sectors have become increasingly dependent on process control systems for their critical operations. To more fully utilize the Matrix for analysis on the nature of consequences of attacks on the various sectors for risk management purposes, more information is needed about how these various sectors are using process control systems and the subsequent interdependencies.

Future FY05 and FY06 activities for NCSD's Control Systems Security Program include efforts to:

- Develop a comprehensive set of control systems security assurance levels for owners and operators;
- Sponsor government/industry workshops to increase awareness among control systems owners and operators of potential cyber incident impacts and vulnerabilities;
- Develop, populate, and validate control systems security scenario assessment tools to provide response teams a web-based application to assess impacts;
- Assess a minimum of three core systems and provide solutions to vulnerabilities and recommendations to protect against cyber threats; and
- Develop the US–CERT CSSC web page for information exchange.

The third major component of NCSD's cyber risk management program is our Software Assurance Program. Software is an essential component of the Nation's critical infrastructure (power, water, transportation, financial institutions, defense industrial base, etc); however, defects in software can be exploited to launch cyber attacks as well as attacks against the critical infrastructure. NCSD developed a comprehensive software assurance framework that addresses people, process, technology, and acquisition throughout the software development lifecycle.

As part of the shared responsibility approach to cyber security, DHS is working to achieve a broader ability to routinely develop and deploy trustworthy software products. As such, DHS is shifting the security paradigm from "patch management" to "software assurance" by encouraging U.S. software developers to raise the bar on software quality and security. In collaboration with other federal agencies, academia, and the private sector, we are:

- Sponsoring the development of a repository of best practices and practical guidance for the software development community;

---

[4] Idaho (INL), Pacific Northwest (PNNL), Los Alamos (LANL), Argonne (ANL), Sandia (SNL), Savannah River (SRNL)

- Developing a software assurance common body of knowledge from which to develop curriculum for education and training;
- Examining recommendations from the Networking and Information Technology Research and Development (NITRD), Software Design and Productivity (SDP), and High Confidence Software and Systems (HCSS) coordination groups and anticipating greater direct engagement with them in the future.
- Facilitating discussions with industry and academic institutions through Software Assurance Forums;
- Collaborating with NIST to inventory software assurance tools and measure effectiveness, identify gaps and conflicts, and develop a plan to eliminate gaps and conflicts;
- Completing the DHS/Department of Defense co-sponsored comprehensive review of the National Information Assurance Partnership (NIAP)[5] with the draft report to be published in September 2005; and
- Promoting investment in applicable software assurance research and development.

DHS will seek to reduce risks by raising the level of trust for all software, minimizing vulnerabilities and understanding threats. DHS will collaborate with government, industry, academic institutions, and international allies to achieve these software assurance objectives.

Another important cyber element of national infrastructure protection is the proliferation of the Internet in our society and daily lives. To mitigate the risks inherent in the rapidly growing user base and increasing usage, NCSD is engaged in a cyber security awareness program that leverages a variety of partners including the National Cyber Security Alliance, the Multi-State ISAC, and the Federal Trade Commission, among others, to reach out to the home user, K–12, small business, and higher education audiences to raise the American public's awareness of cyber risks and security measures.

**Research and Development for Cyber Security and Critical Infrastructure Protection**

Cyber-related research and development (R&D) is vital to improving the resiliency of the Nation's critical infrastructures. This difficult strategic challenge requires a coordinated and focused effort from across the Federal Government, State and local governments, the private sector, and academia to advance the security of critical cyber systems.

A critical area of focus for DHS is the development and deployment of technologies to protect the Nation's cyber infrastructure, including the Internet and other critical infrastructures that depend on IT systems for their mission. Two components within DHS share responsibility for cyber R&D, with the Science & Technology (S&T) Directorate serving as the primary agent responsible for executing cyber security R&D programs. NCSD has responsibility for developing requirements for DHS' cyber security R&D projects.

The S&T Directorate's mission is to conduct, stimulate, and enable research, as well as to develop, test, evaluate, and transition homeland security capabilities to federal, State and local operational end-users. The goals of the DHS S&T Directorate's Cyber Security R&D program are to:

- Perform R&D aimed at improving the security of existing deployed technologies and to ensure the security of new emerging systems;
- Develop new and enhanced technologies for the detection of, prevention of, and response to cyber attacks on the Nation's critical information infrastructure; and
- Facilitate the transfer of these technologies into the national infrastructure as a matter of urgency.

NCSD supports the overall DHS R&D mission by identifying areas for cyber innovation and coordinating with S&T. NCSD collects, develops, and submits cyber security R&D requirements to provide input to the federal cyber security R&D commu-

[5] The National Information Assurance Partnership, established in August of 1997, is a joint effort between NIST and NSA to provide technical leadership in security-related information technology test methods and assurance techniques. NIAP uses the Common Criteria to evaluate and certify commercial off the shelf (COTS) products. There has been much discussion in past years on the effectiveness (time and cost) of the NIAP process. As a result, the National Strategy to Secure Cyberspace recommended an independent review of the program be conducted to make recommendations for its improvement.

nity and specifically to inform the DHS S&T Directorate's cyber security research priorities.

DHS S&T's Cyber Security Research and Development Center is currently working on several projects that support the recommendations of the National Strategy to Secure Cyberspace, while addressing the vulnerabilities of critical systems and infrastructures. The major areas are:

- Working with industry to develop secure routing protocols for the core of the Internet.
- Development of a cyber security test bed for researchers and developers.
- Establishment of a large database of anonymized data collected from the Internet to support research on new cyber security tools and techniques.
- Partnering with the government of Canada on a joint experiment involving the handheld BlackBerry data devices for secure communications between first responders.
- Funding research on understanding and countering emerging Internet threats.
- Funding small business innovative research in the development of new cyber security products.
- Coordination with the Institute for Information Infrastructure Protection (I3P) on the development of new technologies for securing SCADA systems and networks and analyzing the economics of cyber security.

To support and document cyber security R&D initiatives across the Federal Government, NCSD participates in the Cyber Security and Information Assurance Interagency Working Group (CSIA IWG), co-chaired by S&T and the Office of Science and Technology Policy (OSTP). Participants include the National Science Foundation (NSF), the Defense Advanced Research Projects Agency (DARPA), the National Institute of Standards and Technology (NIST) and many others. By reporting to both the Infrastructure Subcommittee and NITRD, the CSIA IWG is positioned to coordinate cyber security and information assurance R&D across agencies, while ensuring that the security of critical infrastructures is emphasized. The CSIA IWG is currently completing the Federal Cyber Security and Information Assurance R&D Plan.

**Moving Forward**

In connection with the National Infrastructure Protection Plan, efforts are underway to assess cyber threats, reduce vulnerabilities and identify significant interdependencies. These efforts will be fully implemented as the SSAs implement their portion of the NIPP. In partnership with NCS and other agencies, we are working through the Internet Disruption Working Group to address the resiliency and recovery of Internet functions in the case of a major cyber incident. We have established a Control Systems Security Program to address core operating systems of critical infrastructure sectors. And, we are working with the government, private sector, and academia to promote the integrity and security of software. We continue to enhance our cyber incident readiness and response system, and we coordinate with our private sector stakeholders to provide protective guidance to our stakeholders through US–CERT. We are conducting a major exercise later this year to test the Cyber Annex to the National Response Plan. Through this effort, we will pull together appropriate entities in the Federal Government, State governments, and appropriate private sector stakeholders to test our capabilities and, subsequently, to improve our incident management process.

We are committed to achieving success in meeting our goals and objectives, but we cannot do it alone. We will continue to meet with industry representatives, our government counterparts, academia, and State representatives to formulate the partnerships needed for productive collaboration and leverage the efforts of all, so we, as a nation, are more secure in cyberspace and in our critical infrastructures.

Again, thank you for the opportunity to testify before you today. I would be happy to answer any questions you may have at this time.

### Biography for Donald A. (Andy) Purdy, Jr.

In October 2004, Donald A. (Andy) Purdy, Jr. was appointed by Secretary Ridge as the Acting Director of the National Cyber Security Division (NCSD) for the Department of Homeland Security, within the Information Analysis and Infrastructure Protection (IAIP) Directorate. The IAIP Directorate identifies and assesses a broad range of intelligence information concerning threats to the people and communities of the United States and to protect the critical infrastructure systems vital to our national security, governance, public health and safety, economy, and national morale.

The NCSD's mission, in cooperation with public, private, and international entities, is to secure cyberspace and America's cyber assets. The key components of this mission involve: (1) implementation of the *National Strategy to Secure Cyberspace and the DHS Strategic Plan;* and (2) implementation of priority protective measures to secure cyberspace and to reduce the cyber vulnerabilities of America's critical infrastructures.

Prior to joining the Department, Mr. Purdy worked on assignment to the White House as Deputy to the Vice Chair and Senior Advisor for IT Security and Privacy to the President's Critical Infrastructure Protection Board (PCIPB) working on the development of the National Strategy to Secure Cyberspace. With the PCIPB, Purdy worked in the areas of cyber crime, privacy protection, government procurement and maintenance of more secure products and systems, security of the financial sector's information systems, and in promoting information sharing in industry sectors such as health care and finance. In April 2003, Mr. Purdy came to the Department where he worked on the cyber tiger team to help design and launch the NCSD in June 2003. Following that he served as Acting Director until Amit Yoran was appointed Director in the Fall of 2003.

Immediately prior to his assignment to the White House staff, Mr. Purdy served as Chief Deputy General Counsel and later as Acting General Counsel for the U.S. Sentencing Commission. The Sentencing Commission is charged with promulgating and updating the Federal Sentencing Guidelines for individuals and organizations, and for providing counsel to the Congress and others about federal sentencing practices and policies. At the Sentencing Commission Mr. Purdy served as a member of the senior management team and provided legal, strategic, administrative, and ethical advice to the Chair and Commissioners, Staff Director and Unit Chiefs.

Mr. Purdy graduated from the College of William and Mary and the University of Virginia Law School. After receiving his law degree, Purdy served as an Assistant Attorney General in Missouri, and then as Senior Staff Counsel to the U.S. House of Representatives Select Committee on Assassinations' investigation of the assassination of President Kennedy. He subsequently served as an Assistant U.S. Attorney in Philadelphia where he concentrated on investigating and prosecuting white collar crime. Following his service as a federal prosecutor, Mr. Purdy returned to Washington, D.C. to serve as Counsel to the U.S. House of Representatives Committee on Standards of Official Conduct (Ethics).

Mr. Purdy then moved to investigative work in network news, working as an Associate Producer for the NBC News magazines *First Camera* and *Monitor,* and then as the Producer for News and Politics for the CBS News broadcast NIGHTWATCH. Subsequently, while at the Sentencing Commission, Mr. Purdy was detailed to Capitol Hill where he worked as Counsel to the U.S. Senate Impeachment Trial Committee for the impeachment trial of then-chief federal judge Walter Nixon of Mississippi.

Mr. Purdy lives in Bethesda, Maryland, with his wife Robin Fader, an Emmy Award winning television and commercial producer, and their daughter, Alexandra, who is 10 years old and has a certified black belt in Tae Kwon Do.

Chairman BOEHLERT. Thank you very much, Mr. Purdy.

Mr. Leggate.

## STATEMENT OF MR. JOHN S. LEGGATE, CHIEF INFORMATION OFFICER AND GROUP VICE PRESIDENT, DIGITAL & COMMUNICATIONS TECHNOLOGY, BP PLC., UNITED KINGDOM

Mr. LEGGATE. Thank you, Mr. Chairman, and thank you, distinguished Members.

My name is John Leggate. I am CIO for BP, and this morning, I also represent BENS, which is Business Executives for National Security in the U.S., a large organization whose interest, of course, is improving the nature of business and its dependency on the Internet.

By way of context, also, BP happens to be the biggest provider of oil and gas in the United States. So, in fact, in our normal business, we take the whole issue of national security as a very, very fundamental part of what we do for the United States.

Anyway, going on from that, this topic, as you said, Mr. Chairman, has actually been in our minds for some time. It has been around, and I think what I would like to do here is point to two things just to simply portray a little bit more of why this is so important today and a few ideas on the way forward above and beyond what is said here.

Almost by stealth since the fail of the dot-com era companies have actually been moving towards the Net progressively. We have done survey work, and our most recent survey would say, in the energy sector, the chemicals and transport sector, up to 30 percent of their revenues come from work done on the Internet today in the United States. In a sense, the dependency is very clear and growing.

And the second point, after Mr. Purdy's point, the nature of business automation regarding running process plants, refineries, and chemical plants are now moving to a place where they look simply like regular computers. They are not different systems anymore. And the capacity for these systems then to be impaired is quite important. In fact, with time, we see a bigger growth in what we call machine-to-machine information flow than simply humans on the Internet, per se. I mean, today, in the world, I think at any point in time, 200 million people are on the Internet with a billion possible connections going on.

So moving on from that to say this is a big issue. The thing that I would note, it isn't simply cyber security but the confluence of cyber and physical security in the Internet. Solving the cyber issue doesn't solve the reliability or the vulnerability of the Internet. There are number of points in the world which are well disclosed where big nodes come together. There are critical points that you can find. If you choose to scan the Internet, you will see these today where it all comes together. And of course, it is—that becomes another big issue as to who is in charge. How should we secure or harden these particular environments?

So another area to think about in all of this conversation is making sure we touch on the edges on the nature of the physical distribution of the Internet. Now you might say, "What are companies doing for themselves in the space, because clearly they should be self-reliant?" And we are pretty well. But in a sense, what we do control, if you like, is the last mile, the mile into our premises. But the millions of miles of Internet, we have no control over and no say-so on its deliverability or its resilience. So all of this traffic is heading to a place where it is almost out of reach of the businesses, but because of economic pressures, efficiency, and almost an always-on environment which we demand nowadays, the job is on.

So that broadly says that the problem is real. It is big and probably getting bigger with time. And the dimensions are not well aware with policy makers. In my job, I travel around most of the world, and I would say the same level of lack of knowledge of the dependency of real business, if you like, world trade is now coming to the Internet.

Look at the United States where we have eight channels of principle critical national infrastructure and trace it all back, most of it ends up somewhere back on the Internet. So if you look through energy, transportation, aviation, it all comes, to some point, to some degree, to the Internet.

And then to look forward more optimistically say what there is to do, I would offer there are two areas to think about. One is fixing what we have. And we have heard from Mr. Purdy various endeavors to do that. I would only add to his remarks and say what business would look at isn't simply the risk envelope but the consequences. Within a major corporation, as in BP, the number of attempts or events per day that come into the system is between a half million and a million attempts on the Internet. Of those, only a handful really matter to the company.

And the issue is how do you screen out the knives on the Internet and get to the issues that actually ultimately take out business and make it quite difficult. So working with that, certainly businesses want to become more aligned with activities of the agencies to bring forward the notion of risk management and consequences into this conversation so that the money is spent wisely on the right priorities. Because you can imagine, you could do a ton of research across a large landscape and not nail the problem.

So the question is how do you converge the issue in the near-term, in the course of 2006, 2007, and 2008 to put this into a much better state? So that is one aspect of the way forward.

I think the other aspect of the way forward is really a new conversation, and I will call it mixed generation Internet, not Internet 2, which is basically in the scientific domain, but looking 20 years out. Most of all, of the United States to start a conversation that moves us to the next generation, if you like, of public utility, i.e., in order so business can progress. Already, in my travels to the Far East, countries like South Korea and Japan are talking of moving to IPv6, and so we are going to end up, at some stage, with different initiatives in different geographies but no one really holding the game plan, the overall strategic intent, or I would call it, technology development map, even the governments. Who gets to say in such a complex world?

So from my point of view, let me summarize and say the issue is real. We should not be distracted into the near-term issues alone, but also take the position, I think, through this committee to discuss what is the nature of the strategic intent for the future that ensures world trade carries on in the way it is.

Thank you, Mr. Chairman.

[The prepared statement of Mr. Leggate follows:]

PREPARED STATEMENT OF JOHN S. LEGGATE

## BUSINESS CONCERNS FOR THE INTERNET

### STATEMENT OF THE ISSUE

The Internet is rapidly becoming the backbone of the world economy. This is particularly true for the United States where the use of the Internet underpins many aspects of the U.S. economy and national critical infrastructure (e.g., energy, water, transportation). Given this fundamental dependency on its continuous availability, the public Internet must be better protected, managed and controlled. In the longer-term, the U.S. should take a leadership role in creating the next generation Global Internet.

**SUMMARY OF THE ISSUE**

The growth of Internet use has been nothing short of extraordinary.[1] Almost by stealth since the dot com collapse, governments, public bodies and large and small scale businesses have been transformed to operate with the Internet as a core piece of business infrastructure. Businesses from all over the world have found the Internet to be a cost effective and reliable business tool. Indeed, in the last few years, in addition to conventional business transactions, many of the controls systems (SCADA) that support national and public utilities are adopting the Internet as a core data transport method.[2] This has resulted in businesses and societies becoming critically dependent on the continuous operation of the Internet.[3]

Businesses have moved from dial-up and dedicated point to point leased lines to committing mission critical digital traffic to operate on the Internet, yet with no practical alternative to maintain business continuity. However, the Internet is mostly run by groups of diverse academic and non-profit organizations which operate via loose consensus. Many governments have apparently not yet fully grasped that national and international economies and their citizens are now dependent on this network of networks—i.e., the global communications backbone.

In its current operation the Internet has well known physical and logical security weaknesses both nationally and globally. What is *not* truly known is the potential business impact of these weaknesses on the U.S. and the world economy. Continued operation is presumed, but is in no way guaranteed. This is compounded by the poor understanding of dependency/interdependencies between companies and critical infrastructures supporting nations/regions.

Global competition has driven the need for ever increasing levels of productivity and innovation from businesses and this has driven the demand for cheaper and more ubiquitous communications. The nature of the architecture of the Internet has allowed it to carry an ever increasing variety of services, with ever decreasing costs. These forces are driving applications, services and business processes from every sector onto the Internet. Businesses that fail to exploit these cost and performance advantages are at a competitive disadvantage.

Today, at moment there are some 200 million individuals active on the Internet. By the end of 2005, at least one billion people will have access to its enormous resources.[4] Also there are as many automated systems—including SCADA systems, CCTV, pipelines, electricity grids, e-mail servers, inventory systems and medical monitoring devices. These systems often communicate over the Internet without human intervention. This machine-to-machine communication is growing dramatically and could supplant interactive use by people in a few years.[5]

In 2004, $6.9 trillion of the $55.6 trillion of worldwide trade was directly transacted over the Internet.[6] Of the remaining trade there was a significant proportion that relied on supporting activity using the Internet for communication—including specification queries, logistics and links between internal processes within companies. Even financial institutions use the Internet for many routine electronic funds transfers.[7] Significantly, in 2004 and in the U.S. alone, 14.8 million high tech jobs relied directly on the Internet.[8]

In the past there have been attempts to address the issues of security, operational stability and reliability but with limited success. For example, work conducted by the President's Commission on Critical Infrastructure Protection (PCCIP) nearly ten years ago, raised vulnerabilities that are apparently yet to be addressed.[9] It set a goal of a reliable, interconnected, and secure information system infrastructure by the year 2003. Is the context and sense of urgency different today?

This paper explains why the context is now so very different. In the '80s and early '90s companies were not using the Internet in anything like the same way or to the same scale as they do today. Private networks were the common means of communication. The companies providing Internet infrastructure were justified in treating identified weaknesses as rather academic and with little economic importance.

However, things have changed and in ways that often only businesses directly using the Internet can articulate.[10] Companies can, and do, take security measures

---

[1] Lazarus Research Group
[2] Internet Security Systems
[3] Jupiter Research
[4] Meta Research
[5] ZDNet Research
[6] Forrester Research, Inc.
[7] Forrester Research, Inc.
[8] University of Texas-Austin
[9] PCCIP Report 1997
[10] See Appendix.

to protect the systems they run and the services directly under their immediate control. But they can do little, to protect the external network infrastructure on which they rely or even engage in a meaningful dialogue about fundamental performance expectations. Previous work in evaluating risks to the Internet has almost entirely focused around a dialogue between supply-side telecommunications/IT companies and government.[11] We therefore only have half the picture, knowledge of interdependency between supply and demand-side for Internet services clearly needs to be shared.

Even more troubling is that many demand-side organizations do not realise how dependent they are on the Internet. Corporations have become linked to the Internet in ways that are not always easily discerned. For example, a major corporation that depends on a third party's logistical services may be surprised to learn that their supplier communicates internal orders and status using the Internet, or that an electric utility they depend upon has moved its process control network to run over the Internet.

These cascading dependencies all too quickly create 'domino effects' that are not obvious to the corporate customer or to the policy-maker. They are usually only discovered during unplanned outages when capabilities begin to degrade or fail in unexpected ways, or are discovered during widely-based crisis management exercises. Businesses and governments can plan for expected failures. But even the best prepared organizations and corporations may be woefully inadequate in responding to complex, low probability, high impact failures. If a large scale Internet outage or significant reduction in performance were to occur, the unexpected effects on whole sets of industries, utilities and enterprise could have surprisingly large economic and societal impacts.

Whether the failure of the Internet arises through error, a worm-writers experiment, or more directed physical or cyber attacks, vulnerabilities exist and this is a real and present risk. Recent reports about "Cyber attack" attempts being developed and the posting of hacker tools with directions on some of the extremist's websites may be warning signs.

**BROADER CONTEXT**

It is worth recalling that the Internet was set up as a government sponsored project, with the U.S. Government as the primary customer and 'anchor tenant.' Its creation was a bold and dramatic step-out that went on to evolve into a remarkable resource that has significantly exceeded the wildest imaginings of its creators. As a result it is being used far beyond anything envisaged in the original designs.

Since its creation, the Internet has developed rapidly in scale, but its technical design has progressed more through steady incremental evolution than through any step change. The "grass roots" and academically-based standards setting process of the Internet Engineering Taskforce (IETF) has had great success. However, the down-side of this consensus approach is that entity wide coordination and alignment is difficult to achieve and step changes are difficult to implement. Internet standards setters are a community of interest and as such they share interests, but they do not share goals and timescales in the way that a project with a clear mandate does.[12]

This diversity of interest has been compounded by the loss of the primary customer, i.e., the U.S. Government, driving operational performance requirements, since they have started to use alternative infrastructures for extra critical services. Instead of a single 'anchor tenant,' the Internet now has countless customers drawn from many governments, corporations and individual users and is thus driven by a very diverse range of agendas, without a clear priority setting process. This will further slow change and adaptation to the new and emerging context of Internet use.

The question we need to ask is whether incremental change will be sufficient to address the current physical and digital integrity weaknesses. The current deficiencies on the Internet may well be filled by tactical repairs, but the potential gap of predictable demand for high volume traffic with high quality services and the intractable vulnerabilities will require a more radical approach. Arguably the risks we are seeing, illustrated by spreading worms and viruses and underlying common mode weaknesses in technologies and physical infrastructure are systemic and sys-

[11] National Security Technology Advisory Committee (NSTAC) and the National Infrastructure Assurance Council (NIAC).

[12] Drawn from I-space theory. Max Boisot, INSEAD.

tematic in nature.[13] Systemic and systematic risks can only be addressed through coordinated rather than isolated action. A fact well illustrated by other complex systems such as vaccination statistics and epidemiology in the medical world and in the risk management intervention required in national and global banking systems.[14] Many of these risks have no geographic or country boundaries—impact and influence is global.

The widespread globalization of the Internet also introduces a further development complexity. Scores of countries now have fundamental interests in its evolution and some are even orchestrating local step-changes in technology.[15] However, no country has yet felt able to propose fundamental change on a global basis. Within the U.S., the Internet is seen in many quarters as the starting point for the National Information Infrastructure (NII). Around the world, there is growing recognition that the set of NIIs (assuming each country commits to developing one) should be compatible with each other in an—as yet—undefined way. Who should take the lead in ensuring this compatibility? There is clearly an important role for government leadership in framing this strategic agenda—with strong collaboration with commerce and business.

In practice, the technical scope of the Internet already goes beyond that defined as "Internet services." Ultimately, the communication pathways must enter the user's machine/other digital devices, pass through layers of software and end up in applications programs. The computer industry, along with the many vendors of computer-related equipment, must play a role in determining how this aspect of the Internet will evolve and therefore form part of the supply-side. A key to the success of the Internet is to ensure that the interested parties have an equitable way of participating in its evolution, including participation in its evolving standards process and technology roadmap. A proper role for governments would be to oversee this process to make sure that it meets the wide spectrum of public and industry needs.

Yet further complexity and dependency is being introduced by a new breed of service providers who are offering services that will continue to supplant alternative networks. Telephony (through Voice Over IP), television, radio and almost all forms of communication are migrating to the Internet or including the Internet as a key component in the communication path.

## CONCLUSIONS ON CURRENT POSITION

- There are no clear accountabilities or guarantees for the continuity of operation of the Internet. Even weaknesses known about for some time have not yet been addressed.
- A significant and growing proportion of the world economy is dependent on the Internet.
- The Internet is currently subject to technical and geopolitical risk and therefore not only the U.S. economy, but economies worldwide, are at risk.
- The U.S. Government itself is no longer fully dependent on the Internet, as it has alternative networks at its disposal for critical services. Thus the Internet has moved from having a single 'anchor tenant' to a diverse community of stakeholders without a voice in the operational performance expectations of the current Internet.
- New technologies and emergent Internet uses, such as Voice Over IP and widespread control system connectivity, are increasing dependency and compounding the risk.

## OPTIONS ON THE WAY FORWARD

We would consider a two-pronged approach, to address both the immediate risk and the strategic opportunity:

### 1. Short-Term

To address immediate concerns a series of in-depth and as necessary classified studies, workshops and truly cross-sectoral exercises should be held to allow businesses (that deliver critical aspects of national infrastructure—e.g., energy, transportation and financial) and governments to share critical information under the *Protected Critical Infrastructure Information (PCII) Program.* The goal of this work

---

[13] Illustrated by work from the Cooperative Association for Internet Data Analysis (www.caida.org).

[14] Drawn from standard epidemiology texts and banking risk texts and the opinions of banking regulators.

[15] For example, the broad introduction of IPv6 in Korea and Japan.

would be to map the business reliance upon the Internet against known areas of risk and develop a priority plan to focus actions that are necessary for increasing its robustness and integrity.

The work could start with the scope of the U.S. economy in a global context. Interdependency should then dictate that it be extended in the first instance to other countries from the G8 and EU.

**2. Medium-Term**

There is a need to create the next generation Internet in a form that would be able to handle the emerging demands of business, civil societies and governments. This would include the technical design necessary to meet physical and logical diversity and resilience. In addition, the program should include the development of a Global Internet Management Framework that addresses broad policies and standards, clarity of operational accountabilities, and technology roadmaps. The goal should be to assure the performance and digital integrity of the new Global Internet, in terms of resilience to physical and cyber-security risks, supplier commercial failure, and broader geopolitical risks.

We believe the U.S. should take a leading role in this proposed global initiative.

Thank you for the opportunity to express the views of the business community. I look forward to continuing our conversation as our CEO roundtable at BENS (Business Executives for National Security) progresses. We look forward to contributing to the actions that we propose.

**APPENDIX**

## Business Criticality Data

Having recognized the potential for serious negative impact on the U.S. critical national infrastructure in the event of a significant interruption of Internet service, a group of concerned business people carried out an informal survey of key sector companies in early 2005. The graph below shows the findings from that survey, indicating the level of dependency these sectors have on the Internet.

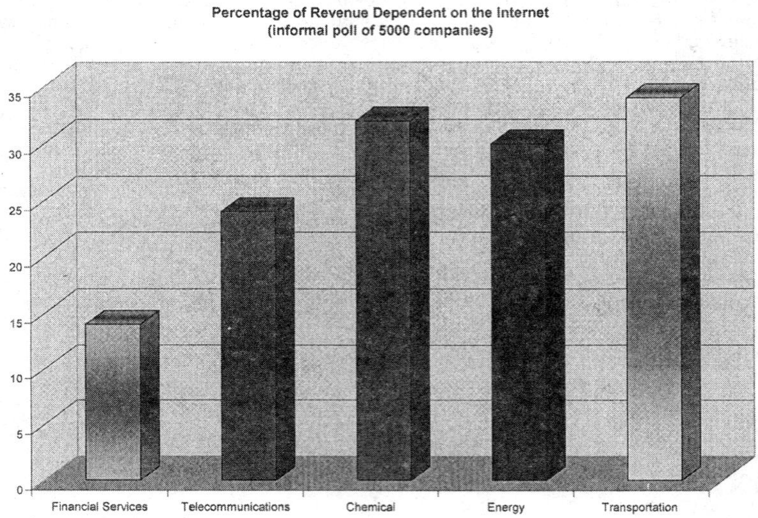

BIOGRAPHY FOR JOHN S. LEGGATE

As CIO of BP, John Leggate is responsible for the development of BP's digital capability—its related systems, technology, business processes and business opportunities—across the company's global operations, Exploration and Production, Refining and Marketing and Trading.

John was elected a Fellow of the Royal Academy of Engineering in July 2005. He was also honored as Commander, The Most Excellent Order of the British Empire (CBE) by the Queen in her 2004 New Year's Honour List. This is in recognition of an outstanding contribution and leadership of the international digital technology agenda.

A chartered engineer, a graduate of Glasgow University and a Fellow of the IEE, began his career in marine consultancy and nuclear energy before joining BP Exploration in 1979. During the 1980–90s he held posts of increasing responsibility in the management and operating of BP's North Sea oil and gas assets.

In 1998, he was appointed President of BP's Azerbaijan International Operating Company, in which capacity he was tasked to manage BP's interests in the unfolding geopolitical and economic debate that centered on crude oil export routes from the Caspian Sea.

John has a particular interest in leadership, the management of high-performance teams and organizational change.

He is married with two children, lives in London and travels widely on behalf of the company.

John S. Leggate CBE FREng.
CIO, GVP Digital & Communications Technology
and GVP Procurement & Supply Chain Management

BP p.l.c.
1 St. James's Square
London
SW1Y 4PD
United Kingdom

6th September, 2005

The Honorable Sherwood Boehlert
Chairman, Science Committee
2320 Rayburn Office Building
Washington, DC 20515

Direct +44 (0)20 7496 5363
Fax +44 (0)20 7496 2393
jslcio@bp.com
www.bp.com

Dear Congressman Boehlert,

Thank you for the invitation to testify before the Committee on Science of the U.S. House of Representatives on Thursday 15th September 2005 for the hearing entitled "Cybersecurity: How Can the Government Help Address Vulnerabilities in Critical Industries?"

In accordance with the Rules Governing Testimony, I confirm that I have received no federal funding directly supporting the subject matter on which I testified, in the current fiscal year or either of the two proceeding fiscal years.

Sincerely,

John S. Leggate

Chairman BOEHLERT. Thank you very much, Mr. Leggate.
Mr. Kepler.

## STATEMENT OF MR. DAVID E. KEPLER, CORPORATE VICE PRESIDENT OF SHARED SERVICES AND CHIEF INFORMATION OFFICER, THE DOW CHEMICAL COMPANY

Mr. KEPLER. Thank you, Chairman Boehlert and Ranking Member Gordon, for allowing me to share my thoughts on this important topic.

Mr. Chairman, before I begin, our thoughts and prayers go out to the millions of Americans, including many of our 7,000 employees, on the Gulf Coast who have lost so much from Hurricane Katrina.

The importance of information infrastructure for communications and emergency response in a national crisis has never been more apparent.

I am Dave Kepler, Corporate Vice President of Shared Services and Chief Information Officer of the Dow Chemical Company, the world's largest chemical and plastics producer.

I am also here as Chairman of the Executive Board of our Industry Cyber Security Program. Our mission is to understand, prioritize, and coordinate our efforts to address cyber security risks.

Today, I would like to discuss the role of information technology in our sector, describe the cyber security threats we face, and highlight what is being done to address these threats. I will also suggest areas where I think government can help.

With $109 billion in exports, the chemical industry is the largest exporter in the U.S. economy. We employ one million Americans and are one of the largest private industry investors in research and development. Our products help keep the water we drink safe, increase productivity of agriculture, enable medical innovations, and are essential to homeland defense and the war on terror.

It is in our nation's interest to have a competitive chemical industry. Information technology is key in maintaining that competitiveness. At Dow, information technology is fully integrated into all aspects of our business, and advanced technology is used to secure our facilities. We rely on the automation and integration of our processes to drive productivity, quality, and safety.

The Internet is a valuable communications tool essential to public safety and emergency response. For example, when all of the phone service was disrupted from the hurricane, Dow was able to use the Internet and Internet-based phones to communicate with our people in the region.

In 2004, chemical industry executives conducted an industry vulnerability assessment. We concluded that, unlike an attack on other critical infrastructures, a security breach from cyber would not cause cascading impact across the chemical industry. However, we believe the highest concern for our industry is the potential of a combined physical and cyber attack.

There are three specific areas for concern in the chemical industry.

One, using information on shipments, product inventory, or sites to construct a physical attack. That is why Dow has set in place practices, policies, and technologies to protect critical plant systems and corporate networks.

Two, using false identity to acquire chemicals for improper use. Our company counters this threat by pre-identifying and verifying customers.

Three, gaining inappropriate access to systems to cause isolated disruptions. At Dow, operating practices and authentication technologies are continuously being upgraded to restrict access based on roles and clearances.

Our company has conducted a comprehensive cyber security risk analysis, and we have used the Sandia National Lab's methodology for assessing vulnerabilities for our sites and manufacturing facilities. Dow has developed a cyber security management plan, and we continue to test and upgrade our plans in all areas of security.

But we cannot address cyber security threats alone. Security of the communications and Internet infrastructure is beyond any one sector's control. Protecting these vital assets from a significant attack, whether physical, cyber, or a combination, is of utmost importance.

So what role does government play?

The Department of Homeland Security must contend with the real threat of attacks by people, organizations, or nations intent on causing significant disruptions to our economy and way of life. Protecting communications in the event of a national emergency must be a priority along with threat monitoring and modeling, authentication methods and information protection. We must understand how to prevent attacks, what is needed to defend against attacks, and how to recover infrastructure from a catastrophic failure. Department of Homeland Security resources and R&D efforts must be dedicated to the big picture.

In closing, we are encouraged by the Department's work to provide—the work with the private sector to reduce vulnerabilities and minimize the severity of cyber attacks. But more needs to be done to share and protect relevant information across all sectors and government. Government crisis management and disaster recovery plans must include industry participation, coordinated emergency response, and ongoing monitoring, and managed recovery efforts with government and industry together are critical.

Thank you, and I will be happy to answer any questions at the end.

[The prepared statement of Mr. Kepler follows:]

PREPARED STATEMENT OF DAVID E. KEPLER

Thank you Chairman Boehlert and Ranking Member Gordon for allowing me to share my thoughts on this important topic.

Mr. Chairman, before I begin, our thoughts and prayers go out to the millions of Americans, including many of our 7,000 employees on the gulf coast who have lost so much from Hurricane Katrina.

Our number one priority is the safety and well-being of our employees and the communities impacted by this disaster. We are committed to safely returning our facilities to full operation and contributing to the recovery efforts. The importance of information infrastructure for communications and emergency response in a national crisis has never been more apparent.

I'm Dave Kepler, Corporate Vice President of Shared Services and Chief Information Officer of The Dow Chemical Company. Dow is the world's largest chemical and plastics producer with annual sales of over $40 billion serving customers in markets such as: food, transportation, health and medicine, personal and home care, and building and construction.

I am also here as the Chairman of the Executive Board of the Chemical Sector Cyber Security Program. This effort was established in 2002 to coordinate the sector's activity and to align with the U.S. Government's National Strategy to Secure Cyberspace. The program's mission is to understand the risks we face as a sector and coordinate and prioritize our efforts to reduce those risks. Leadership for this program is provided by the chemical industry's leading CIOs, and leverages expertise from existing organizations: chemical trade associations, the Chemical Industry Data Exchange, and the Chemical Sector Information Sharing and Analysis Center.

The five strategic elements of the program are:

- Broad support and participation throughout the sector
- Engagement with government to ensure effective measures to secure cyberspace
- Identification and reduction of infrastructure vulnerabilities to guard against cyber attacks and speed recovery from incidents
- Establishment of management practices and guidance to support overall sector cyber security
- Ongoing coordination with technology providers, government and academia to accelerate development of improved, cost-effective solutions.

The program produced comprehensive cyber security guidance which was built into the Responsible Care Security Code in 2004. Implementation of the Responsible Care Security Code is mandatory for all members of the American Chemistry Council and has also been adopted by the Synthetic Organic Chemical Manufacturers Association.

Our sector continues to work closely with the Department of Homeland Security, standards bodies such as the National Institute of Standards and Technology (NIST) and industry organizations such as Instrumentation Systems and Automation (ISA) to share the latest best practices and to develop new standards to defend against cyber attacks.

Today, I would like to discuss the role of information technology in our sector, describe the cyber security threats we face and highlight what is being done to address these threats. I will also suggest areas where the government can help.

Let me begin by outlining the importance of our sector to our nation's economic well-being and security—enabling 25 percent of our nation's GDP. With $109 billion dollars in exports, the chemical industry is the largest exporter in the U.S. economy. We employ one million Americans and are one of the largest private industry investors in research and development. Our industry makes modern life possible, from plastics to pharmaceuticals, from cars to clothing. Our products help keep the water we drink safe, increase productivity of agriculture, and enable medical innovations that prevent and treat disease. Our industry is also essential to homeland defense and the war on terror—making products that go into bullet-resistant vests, night vision goggles and stealth aircraft.

Our industry's safety culture and history of cooperative voluntary initiatives, partnerships with local, State and Federal Government agencies, and strong support for research and development, position us well to address new security challenges. For example, the industry joined forces to develop the American Chemistry Council's Responsible Care Security Code—building upon long-standing industry safety and emergency response programs.

All aspects of security are integrated into the Security Code including physical plant security, transportation security, as well as cyber security. Implementation of the Responsible Care Security Code is mandatory for all American Chemistry Council members leading to over $2 billion in investments to improve security and preparedness across our industry.

Cyber security has been on our radar screen long before the tragic events of 9/11. At Dow, for example, we have had policies and practices in place for securing our information assets for many years. These cover the use of the Internet, integration of systems, and automation of manufacturing control. The emergence of a significant terrorist threat with the events of 9/11 added urgency and focus to our efforts. It was this event that prompted the establishment of the Chemical Sector Cyber Security program.

It's in our national interest to have a competitive chemical industry, and information technology is key in maintaining that competitiveness. At Dow, information technology is fully integrated into all aspects of our business—research and development, manufacturing, accounting, logistics and sales to name just a few. We also use information technology to interact with government agencies and to report our regulatory compliance. Advanced technology is also being leveraged to secure our facilities and the distribution of our products. We rely on automation and integration of our processes to drive productivity, quality, and safety.

At Dow, approximately 15 percent of our orders are via the Internet, and nearly all of our customers use the Internet to learn about our products, track orders, and get technical support. The Internet is also a valuable communications tool—essential to public safety and emergency response. For example, in the aftermath of Katrina when all phone service was disrupted, Dow was able to use Internet based phones to communicate with our facilities in the region.

In 2004, chemical company executives conducted an industry-level vulnerability assessment to determine the potential impact of cyber security threats. We concluded that, unlike an attack on other critical infrastructures, a cyber security breach would not cause cascading impact across the chemical industry.

We believe the higher concern for our industry is the potential of a combined physical and cyber attack or the criminal use of illegally obtained information.

There are three specific areas of concern for the chemical industry:

1. Using information on shipments, product inventory, or sites to construct a physical attack. That's why Dow has set in place policies, practices and technologies to protect the linkage of critical plant systems with corporate networks.
2. Using false identity to acquire chemicals for improper use. Our company counters this threat by pre-identifying and verifying our customers before electronic orders.
3. Gaining inappropriate access to systems to cause isolated disruptions. At Dow, operating practices and authentication technology is continuously being upgraded to restrict what people can do based on roles and clearances.

For obvious reasons, I cannot get into all we do to protect ourselves, but here are some additional steps that Dow has taken to combat these threats.

Addressing people, process and technology, we have:

- Developed a company-wide cyber security management plan that includes incident management and business continuity.
- Completed a comprehensive cyber security risk analysis based on the ISO information security standard, ISO/IEC 17799.
- Used the U.S. Government Sandia National Labs methodology for assessing vulnerability of our sites and manufacturing facilities—including a review of physical, process, and cyber vulnerabilities.

We continue to test and upgrade our plans in all areas of security.

Although much has been done within the chemical sector, we cannot address cyber security threats alone. Security of the Nation's telecommunications and Internet infrastructure is beyond any one sector's control. Protecting the Nation's critical communication and information infrastructure from a significant attack, whether physical, cyber, or combined, is of the utmost importance.

So, what role should the government play? While there are many issues impacting secure computing today such as random hacking and the e-mail virus of the day, the Department of Homeland Security must contend with the real threat of attacks by people, organizations or nations—intent on causing significant disruption to our economy and way of life. Targeted attacks that could have a major economic or social impact must be the priority as well as protecting our communications capability in the event of a national emergency.

Department of Homeland Security resources and research and development efforts should be dedicated to addressing these 'big picture' threats to benefit all sectors and improve our national security. Threat monitoring and modeling, better methods for authenticating identity, and information protection should be research priorities. Efforts should include understanding how to prevent attacks, what resources and tools are needed to defend against attacks, and what it would take to reconstitute our information technology infrastructure in the event of a catastrophic failure.

We are encouraged by the Department's work with the public and private sectors to reduce vulnerabilities and minimize the severity of cyber attacks. But, more needs to be done around the sharing and protection of relevant information across all critical sectors and government. Finally, government crisis management and disaster recovery plans must include industry participation. As witnessed in the aftermath of Katrina—coordinated emergency response, ongoing monitoring, and managed recovery efforts with government and industry are critical.

We believe continued and expanded cooperation between our critical sector, the Department of Homeland Security and other government agencies as well as information technology providers is vital to reduce vulnerabilities and enhance preparedness.

Any efforts to improve cyber security must:

- Start and end with the commitment to be a risk-based, outcome-focused program. DHS must focus on the real threat of criminal attacks by people, organizations or nations.
- Recognize that cyber security is an integral part of overall security, and build upon the work to date of the chemical sector security programs such as the Responsible Care Security Code and the Chemical Sector Cyber Security Program.
- Recognize the high degree of integration of the chemical sector with other critical infrastructure sectors, as well as the importance of our industry to our homeland defense and economic security.

In closing, we are committed to ensuring the security of our company and to taking a leadership role in improving overall security across our industry. Information sharing and continued cooperation between our sector and the Department of Homeland Security is critical. Above all else, efforts must be focused on those threats of greatest impact and concern to our national security, while addressing the unique needs of each sector.

Thank you and I'd be happy to answer any questions.

## Biography for David E. Kepler

D.E. (Dave) Kepler is Corporate Vice President of Shared Services and Chief Information Officer (CIO) of The Dow Chemical Company. In this capacity, Kepler has global responsibility for Customer Service, Information Systems, Purchasing, Six Sigma, Supply Chain and Work Process Improvement. He is also a member of the Office of the Chief Executive (OCE).

Kepler joined Dow in 1975 in the Western Division Computer and Process Systems group. After progressive Commercial and Information Systems roles throughout the United States, Canada and the Pacific, he was named Director of Chemicals and Plastics Information Systems in 1993. In 1995, Kepler assumed additional responsibility as Director of Global Information Systems Applications. He was appointed Vice President and CIO in February 1998, and in 2000, assumed the role of Corporate Vice President of eBusiness. In 2002, Kepler undertook commercial responsibility for the Advanced Electronic Materials business and further expanded his role the following year, adding responsibility for Global Purchasing and Supply Chain. Kepler assumed his most recent role in January 2004.

Kepler serves on the Board of Directors of the U.S. Chamber of Commerce. He is a member of the American Chemical Society and the American Institute of Chemical Engineers. In addition, he leads the Executive Committee of the Chemical Sector Cyber Security Program. Locally, Kepler serves on the Board of Directors for the Midland Community Cancer Services and Alden B. Dow Museum of Science and Art. He was the 2004 United Way of Midland County Campaign Chair.

Kepler received a Bachelor's degree in chemical engineering from the University of California at Berkeley.

The Dow Chemical Company
Midland, Michigan 48674

September 9, 2005

The Honorable Sherwood Boehlert
Chairman, Science Committee
US House of Representatives
2320 Rayburn Office Building
Washington, DC 20515

Dear Chairman Boehlert:

Thank you for the invitation to testify before the Committee on Science of the U.S. House of Representatives on September 15th for the hearing entitled "***Cybersecurity: How Can the Government Help Address Vulnerabilities in Critical Industries?***" In accordance with the Rules Governing Testimony, this letter serves as formal notice of the federal funding I currently receive related to the hearing topic.

I received no federal funding directly supporting the subject matter on which I testified, in the current fiscal year or either of the two proceeding fiscal years.

Sincerely,

David E. Kepler, II
Corporate Vice President Shared Services
Chief Information Officer
The Dow Chemical Company

Chairman BOEHLERT. Thank you very much, Mr. Kepler.
Mr. Freese.

**STATEMENT OF MR. GERALD S. FREESE, DIRECTOR OF ENTERPRISE INFORMATION SECURITY, AMERICAN ELECTRIC POWER**

Mr. FREESE. Mr. Chairman and distinguished Members of this committee, thank you for the opportunity to appear before you today.

My name is Gerry Freese, Director of Enterprise Information Security at American Electric Power. I am also here representing the North American Electrical Reliability Council in Princeton, New Jersey.

AEP is the largest provider of electricity in the country with over five million customers in 11 states, and I am responsible for information security for all corporate and operational systems and networks, including those used in the operation of the bulk power system.

Before I address the three questions posed to the presenters, I would like to preface my remarks.

In the aftermath of Hurricane Katrina, we have seen the suffering and the unprecedented devastation in Louisiana and Mississippi. We have seen the confusion and chaos when essential services were no longer functioning. We have seen how critical infrastructure can be destabilized and destroyed when links are broken in its complex chain of multiple interdependencies. Whether the cause is a natural disaster or a terrorist attack, the impact on people and the economy is horrendous.

Critical infrastructure industries, by virtue of their interdependencies, have a responsibility to work across all sectors, and this includes the Federal Government, to mitigate risk, ensure service continuity and an expeditious recovery in the event of a natural or manmade disaster.

This hearing is timely in its intent to explore means to expand the cooperation and collaboration between the private and public critical infrastructure sectors.

Now for responses to the three questions.

For the first question, the electricity sector has, in many cases, developed its own telecommunications network for conducting electricity operations, but it is steadily becoming more reliant on public networks. The electric sector uses these public networks for many functions with the net result that its interfaces with the telecommunications sector have become more numerous and complex. Both sectors are working together to better understand their levels of operational integration and in ways the vulnerability in either of these sectors impacts the other.

Because of these complex and critical interdependencies, it is fairly clear that serious damage or disruption of telecommunications could seriously undermine the operation and reliability of the electricity infrastructure. Accordingly, the electric sector has taken some decisive steps to secure the cyber and physical resources and will continue to invest in comprehensive and effective security measures. We have interim cyber security standards in place right now and are working diligently to move through the approval process for a permanent, more expansive critical infrastructure protection standard.

The final product will strengthen cyber security across the electric sector and lay the groundwork for greater collaboration between industry and government.

In response to the second question, the electric industry views government entities, such as DHS and DOE, as partners in sector cyber security. In fact, we have worked extensively with DHS, DOE representatives, the National Labs, and others to try and identify areas of focus for good security and determine means to carry out what we all see as primary responsibilities for national security.

We believe the office of the Assistant Secretary for Cyber Security and Telecommunications should focus on several specific areas covering private and public sector cooperation. These areas center on greater awareness of critical infrastructure interdependencies, information sharing between government and the private sector, and true, non-prescriptive partnerships. I would be happy to elaborate on those three points in the question-and-answer period, if it is possible.

As to the third question regarding possible research and development opportunities, the electric sector is interested in continuing to work closely with DOE on the work being done at the Idaho National Lab. We believe it holds great promise as one of the best and most efficient means of stimulating research and developing technical solutions to the present cyber security problems. DOE and DHS have provided leadership and support on this initiative, and the electricity industry is committed to its success.

Regarding inadequacies of the electric sector security solution, the present electric infrastructure has been built over many years and various types of process control systems produced by a diverse set of vendors. These legacy systems are a large part of the reason that new technology security solutions cannot be more widely deployed across the industry.

The long-term solution to this is to begin a process of rebuilding the old infrastructure with the ultimate goal of replacing it with next-generation equipment and technology. The new infrastructure would be based on greater levels of security and reliability with enhanced design recognition of the interdependencies between the electric and telecommunications sectors.

Work is already underway in this area. The Telecommunications and Electric Power Interdependencies Task Force is exploring the next generation of public networks and how the electricity sector will be able to use these networks of the future through the employment of more sophisticated encryption technology and other security measures.

Cyber security is evolving rapidly, and all of us working in the discipline are tirelessly seeking more effective solutions for protecting our critical assets and systems. We appreciate your interest in this topic and welcome your assistance in helping us to ensure our critical infrastructures are protected, secure, and reliable.

Thank you for your attention.

[The prepared statement of Mr. Freese follows:]

PREPARED STATEMENT OF GERALD S. FREESE

Mr. Chairman and distinguished Members of this committee, thank you for the opportunity to appear before you today. My name is Gerry Freese. I am the Director of Enterprise Information Security for the American Electric Power Company in Columbus, Ohio. AEP is the largest supplier of electricity in the country, with over five million customers in 11 states. I am responsible for information security for all of AEP's corporate and operational systems and networks, including those used for the operation of the bulk electric system.

My reason for being here today is to talk about the cyber security needs and activities of the entire electricity sector, one of North America's most critical infrastructures. During my career, I have worked with numerous industry-wide committees addressing the growing need for increased security for information and cyber systems. This need is underscored by the sheer expanse and diversity of the electricity sector, which is made up of large and small entities, publicly, privately, and government owned and operated. Through industry groups and as individual companies, we have always placed great emphasis and the highest priority on the need to protect our information systems and effectively secure the data residing on them.

Before I address the three questions posed to the presenters by the Committee, I want to make two points.

First, our industry has long-term and positive working relationships with federal agencies, including the Department of Homeland Security (DHS) and the Department of Energy (DOE). We value these relationships and want to work collaboratively to improve them even further. The recent recognition from DOE and DHS of the Electricity Sector Coordinating Council (ESCC) is a positive step. We firmly believe the relationships between federal agencies and the industry are working well because both the electricity sector and the federal agencies recognize the value in jointly addressing issues. Both the industry and government recognize the difficulties posed by prescriptive mandates and overly rigid rules and regulations that stifle creative solutions to problems.

Second, our industry continues to have concerns about the security of information after it is provided to the government. The electric infrastructure is one of the most critical infrastructures servicing the Nation and allowing us to maintain our way of life. Certain technical, architectural and operational aspects and details must be kept secure so they will not be inadvertently disclosed to those who would try to disrupt or destroy our social, political or economic fabric. We believe the Critical Infrastructure Information (CII) approach meets most of the needs for critical information protection but have been frustrated by an evident lack of progress in fully implementing this important safeguard.

I will now respond to the three questions posed by the committee. In response to the first question, the electricity sector has, in many cases, built its own telecommunications networks but is steadily becoming more reliant on public networks as well. The electricity sector uses the public networks for many functions including customer service and information exchange via the Internet. It also uses the Internet and the public networks for a limited amount of telemonitoring of the electrical system, although this varies by individual electric company. The interdependencies between the telecommunications sector and the electricity sector are numerous and complex. Because of these complex and critical interdependencies, serious damage or disruption of the telecommunications infrastructure would seriously undermine the operation and operability of the electricity infrastructure. Both sectors are working together to better understand their criticality and the ways that vulnerabilities in either of these sectors impacts the other.

Securing the extensive, distributed and critical electric power infrastructure is a huge responsibility that the electricity industry takes very seriously. We have already taken decisive steps to secure our cyber and physical resources and will continue to invest in comprehensive and effective security measures. We have interim cyber security standards in place and are working diligently to move through the approval process a permanent, more expansive Critical Infrastructure Protection (CIP) standard. The permanent standard will strengthen cyber security across the electricity sector and lay the groundwork for greater collaboration between the industry and government.

In response to the second question, DHS can assist the electricity sector in cyber security by continuing its support of security activities like Carnegie Mellon's Computer Emergency Readiness team. DHS also has been very supportive of other information sharing activities, which adds value to our industry's security initiatives. Another more recent example is the Process Control Security Forum. This group is made up of several key industry sectors that use process control systems and includes government representatives, academics, and vendors. The forum is working to develop design guidelines for the next generation of more secure control systems and is looking at what can be done to improve existing systems. As the forum continues to make progress, the possibility of seed money from DHS should be considered to stimulate the implementation of the ideas and concepts developed.

Another way that DHS can assist the electricity sector is by helping coordinate research initiatives taking place in cyber security. Many of the most prestigious institutions in America are engaged in research and development in this area. The missing element that hinders real progress is an overall coordination plan to avoid competition for funding and duplication of effort. The coordination should extend beyond the borders of the United States because a number of other countries such as Australia, Canada, Great Britain, and Japan have also made cyber security a top priority.

The third question focused on current inadequacies in security and possible research and development opportunities. The electricity industry is interested in continuing to work closely with DOE on the work being done at the Idaho National Laboratory. We believe it holds great promise as one of the best and most efficient means of stimulating research and developing technical solutions to the present shortfalls in cyber security. DOE and DHS have provided leadership and support on this initiative and the electricity industry is committed to its success. Again,

DHS should coordinate this work with other projects in this topic, both domestically and internationally.

The present electric infrastructure has been built over many years with various types of process control systems produced by a large number of vendors. The long-term solution to present inadequacies is to build out the old infrastructure with the next generation of technologies and equipment. The new infrastructure will be based on greater levels of security and reliability, enhanced design, and recognition of the interdependencies between the electricity sector and the communications sector. Very interesting work is already taking place in this area. The Telecommunications and Electric Power Interdependencies Task Force is exploring the next generation of public networks and how the electricity sector will be able to use these networks of the future through the employment of more sophisticated encryption and other security measures.

The cyber security arena is evolving rapidly and all of us working in the field find it to be an exciting and stimulating professional challenge. Operational and security technologies are changing quickly. We appreciate your interest in the topic and welcome your assistance in helping us to ensure that our critical infrastructures are protected and secure well in the future. Thank you for your attention.

## Biography for Gerald S. Freese

Gerald Freese is the Managing Director of Enterprise Information Security at American Electric Power. He is responsible for defining, developing and executing all information security programs to effectively protect AEP data and systems, including critical digital control systems. He is responsible for regulatory compliance and critical infrastructure protection for cyber security, and has been instrumental in the development of cyber security standards for the energy industry. Gerald Freese is a recognized security and infrastructure protection expert who brings a powerful combination of leadership, domain experience, technological vision and strategy development to American Electric Power. He is the company's primary data security architect, and a strong proponent of industry and government partnerships for critical infrastructure protection.

Prior to accepting a position at American Electric Power, Mr. Freese was the Director of Security Intelligence at Vigilinx, Inc., where he developed an early warning and data analysis process to identify computer-based threats and attack profiles. He has authored in depth analytical papers on cyber-activities relative to geopolitical threat environments and has testified before congress on critical infrastructure interdependencies and control system security. Mr. Freese is a retired naval Cryptologic Officer with extensive experience in computer security and information warfare. He has held other leadership positions in the information technology industry with Perot Systems and General Dynamics Advanced Information Systems.

Mr. Freese is a Certified Information Systems Security Professional (CISSP). He holds a Bachelor's degree from State University of New York (Albany), and a Master's degree in Information and Telecommunications Systems from Johns Hopkins University in Baltimore, Maryland.

September 13, 2005

The Honorable Sherwood Boehlert
Chairman, Science Committee
2320 Rayburn Office Building
Washington, DC 20515

Dear Congressman Boehlert:

Thank you for the invitation to testify before the Committee on Science of the U.S. House of Representatives on September 15th for the hearing entitled "***Cybersecurity: How Can the Government Help Address Vulnerabilities in Critical Industries?***." In accordance with the Rules Governing Testimony, this letter serves as formal notice of the federal funding I currently receive related to the hearing topic.

> I received no federal funding directly supporting the subject matter on which I testified, in the current fiscal year or either of the two proceeding fiscal years.

Sincerely,

Gerald S. Freese

Chairman BOEHLERT. Thank you very much.

Mr. Geisse. After that wonderful introduction by Mr. Akin, I want to make sure we hear you.

**STATEMENT OF MR. ANDREW M. GEISSE, CHIEF INFORMATION OFFICER, SBC SERVICES, INC.**

Mr. GEISSE. It doesn't go against my five minutes, does it?

Okay. Thank you, Chairman Boehlert, Ranking Member Gordon, other Members of the Committee. And I would like to thank Congressmen Akin and Sessions for that unexpected and kind introduction.

I am pleased to represent SBC Communications on this panel focused on cyber security within critical industries.

SBC has a long history of providing reliable communication services. We provide voice and data communication services as a local exchange carrier in 13 states. We also provide services nationally as a long distance provider, data services provider, and Internet services. We have a national wireless presence with BellSouth in

Cingular Wireless, and we recognize the importance of our nation's critical communications infrastructure and the role that it plays for the security of the United States and its citizens. Integrity and reliability of our networks have been cornerstones of the communications industry.

At SBC, we implement both physical and cyber security measures that protect both our customer-serving networks as well as our internal information systems networks. Physical security measures include things like guard services, card key IDs, visible badge policies, video monitoring, and in special cases, biometric type security.

Information security, though, begins with the employee, and it begins as being part of our code of business conduct that every employee has to read and sign off on each year. We segment our internal network connections from our external network connections using various security technologies to ensure the integrity of our networks. We keep our internal core business network separate from the general employee network, and we use virus protection software, of course, on all of our PCs as well as our e-mail servers.

Proactive vulnerability scanning is a key part of our strategy, and it is something that we do on a daily basis. SBC maintains close ties to government agencies responsible for national security. We work closely with them on a daily basis to receive and share security-related information. Examples are the National Security Telecommunications Advisory Council, the National Coordinating Center Telecom Information Sharing and Analysis Center, Infragard, and the National Security Information Exchange.

Continued government focus on security standards and collaborative support organizations is seen positively by SBC; providing research assistance, grants, and funds to focus the information technology industry to work towards security standards and best practices is absolutely necessary. It is important that the government provides to the critical industries that are part of our infrastructure the best practices that they learn from their own cyber security agencies.

Society in the 21st century is rapidly changing with increasing reliance on information technologies. Users expect that they be mobile and that they have access to the Internet and e-mail wherever they are. Providing secure services in the environment becomes increasingly important and challenging. Federal programs could help educate and assist consumers to understand their roles and responsibilities in a connected world.

As recognized by the Department of Homeland Security, the Nation is dependent on the critical infrastructure of communications, banking and finance, power, food, health, information technology, and others. A disruption to any component of those affects the whole infrastructure. Securing against disruptions of any component is a best interest of all of us.

The communication industry is also increasingly dependent on application and information technology vendors to ensure the products they provide are of the highest quality and integrity. Software and hardware that does not meet industry standards or best practices require additional efforts and expense to meet its expected function. Vendors that provide software or hardware with security vulnerabilities that must be continually monitored, reviewed, patched drain on a company's resources and a liability to companies that must ensure the integrity of their own systems, data, and services.

As a result, cyber security must become a priority in the creation of new information technologies. To date, security components are often an afterthought. I mean, you can look at cellular and Wi-fi when they first came out in the ability to intercept calls, clone phones, and data snooping where they could occur.

Internet protocol-based services wrestle constantly with the need to traverse the same network paths where unscrupulous persons may have the ability to interfere, impede, or intrude on the service itself. IP-based services must find new ways to protect the content of each packet that is carried and delivered in the shared Internet world. SBC is committed to work with the information industry to help build the next generation of Internet-based voice and video and data services securely.

Mr. Chairman and Members of the Committee, your assistance to focus industry attention on cyber security is greatly appreciated. We encourage the Department of Homeland Security to continue to support research grants and assistance that focus on national cyber security, to support industry organizations and government agencies that create security standards and best practices, to continue to provide early warnings of security events through various government agencies, and to make sure that the government-identified security best practices are shared with our private, critical infrastructure industries.

I would like to add that you make sure that our laws carry serious penalties for cyber security issues and that the instigators are prosecuted to the full extent of the law. It must become a major crime. It is no longer just kids playing with computers. It is a real threat and the attacks are serious.

Thank you for the opportunity to appear here today. The work you are doing is critical to our future as a nation. Cyber terrorism is a real threat, and we must stay diligent.

Thank you, Mr. Chairman.

[The prepared statement of Mr. Geisse follows:]

## Prepared Statement of Andrew M. Geisse

Thank you, Chairman Boehlert, Ranking Member Gordon and Members of the Committee.

I am pleased to represent SBC Communications on this panel focused on cyber security within our nation's critical industries.

SBC has a long history of providing reliable communication services. SBC provides voice and data communications services as a local exchange carrier within thirteen states and nationally with long distance, data and Internet services. We also have a national wireless presence in Cingular Wireless in a partnership with BellSouth. We recognize the importance of our nation's critical communication infrastructure and the role it plays for the protection of the United States and its citizens. Integrity and reliability of our networks have been historic cornerstones of the communications industry.

As society becomes more and more dependent on information technology, cyber security must be a priority to protect the services provided by those same resources.

**How does the communications sector depend on public and private information systems?**

SBC well understands the strong connection between communications security and information technology, or what is commonly referred to as cyber security.

Behind the networks that move voice and data, are many applications, private networks, and computing resources. These resources support the operations, administration, maintenance, and provisioning services of our telecommunications infrastructure. These information systems and networks provide SBC and other carriers the ability to manage this complex industry supporting the dial tone and Internet connections that we have all come to expect as a part of our daily lives. Securing these cyber resources to ensure the integrity and availability of communications networks is a role that SBC takes seriously, as part of its corporate culture.

SBC uses many vendor products within its information technology infrastructure. In that regard, SBC is dependent on vendor product development in the private sector and delivery of private sector services and materials to support the information technology services of the infrastructure. In this manner, SBC relies on vendors to incorporate cyber security best practices, standard interfaces, and administrative tools within their products. SBC is also reliant on vendors to ensure their software products can be patched easily to prevent existence of long-term vulnerabilities.

In support of the private sector, SBC provides managed security services as a product offering. These types of services include: risk reviews and analysis, firewall installation and monitoring, and firewall and intrusion prevention/detection reseller for other vendor products.

For the consumer space, SBC's Internet Services organization through our relationship with Yahoo! provides security tools to our Internet Services customers as part of their Internet experience. In this manner, SBC supports cyber security to the consumer so they can better protect their home information technologies, which in turn provides less problems to the shared Internet space.

Other areas where SBC has focused on consumer cyber security is as a founding member of the Internet NOC Hotline, which connects key U.S. and International ISPs. SBC is also a founding member of the Global Infrastructure Alliance for Internet Security.

An area where SBC would recommend government focus is on the education of the consumers regarding cyber security matters. End users must recognize they are part of the interconnected world. When end-users do not understand how virus and worm propagation can impact their home PCs, the result is a negative effect at the Internet level. This impact is caused through a variety of malicious activities, including, SPAM e-mails and bot-networks. Educational awareness programs should advise users on anti-virus protection and identity theft protection.

**What steps is SBC taking to secure its systems?**

At SBC, we implement physical and cyber security measures that protect both our customer-serving network facilities and our internal information services. Physical security measures include guard services, card key technologies, visible badge policies, video monitoring, and, in special cases, bio-metric technologies.

Information security begins with a cyber security policy that is part of our Corporate Code of Business Conduct. We segment our internal network connections from external networks using various security technologies to ensure the integrity of our network. We keep our internal core business networks separate from the general employee network. Virus protection software is deployed as standard on desktops and e-mail servers. Pro-active vulnerability scanning is performed constantly to identify potential areas of risk.

SBC maintains close ties to government agencies responsible for national security. We work closely with them on a daily basis to receive and share security related information. Examples are the National Security Telecommunications Advisory Council (NSTAC), National Coordinating Center Telecom Information Sharing and Analysis Center (NCC Telecom ISAC), Infragard, and the National Security Information Exchange (NSIE).

Internally, SBC has several organizations dedicated to the security of our assets. Organizations such as our National Security/Emergency Preparedness organization, our Asset Protection organization, and our Corporate Information Security organization, work to protect our customers information and services, our employees, and our internal networks and data on a daily basis.

Our SBC Labs business unit works closely with technology vendors, academic communities, and government standards organizations, to partner and share information on new technologies. Cyber security standards are always a priority in future service and technology development and a focus of our internal auditing organization as well as external security audits.

Continued Government focus on security standards and collaborative support organizations is seen positively by SBC. Providing research assistance, grants, and funds to focus the information technology industry to work towards security standards and best practices is necessary. It is important that the Government provides to the critical infrastructure industries the learnings and best practices that its cyber security agencies learn.

Legislation should not always be necessary to bring industry attention to technical priorities. However, providing research assistance, grants, and funds to focus the information technology industry to work towards security standards and best practices is necessary.

**What are the possible consequences for the communication sector of disruption or attack on information systems?**

Society in the 21st century is rapidly changing with increasing reliance on information technologies. Users' expectations are that they be mobile and have instant access to the Internet and their e-mail. Providing secure services in this environment becomes increasingly important and challenging. Federal programs could help educate and assist consumers to understand their roles and responsibilities in a connected world.

To illustrate: Consider how often people stop for gas and use a payment card at the pumps for convenience. The payment card transactions must be carried efficiently, reliably, and securely across communications networks. This is to ensure the gas vendor, the payment card vendor, and the customer are all satisfied that the transaction occurred to everyone's expectation.

The networks, the applications, and the information systems that are necessary to complete transactions of this nature are part of our society on a daily basis. Cyber security is necessary to ensure the integrity of those transactions. Disruptions within the communications sector can impact these, and other, daily activities.

Consider the impact of disrupted or unreliable communications to everyday needs, including how patients obtain collaborative health care between multiple providers and locations. Communications plays ever increasing importance to health industries, emergency first responders, 911 services, law enforcement, banking, power, and other parts of our society that serve critical functions.

With the growing use of wireless technologies, we must recognize that those wireless systems still rely on an underlying physical transport, use of back-end systems and applications that may interconnect with other carriers. As we have recently witnessed in New Orleans and the Gulf Coast, if the supporting infrastructure is disrupted, communication fails. A cyber disruption could cause similar impacts as a physical disruption.

While we recognize that other critical infrastructure industries are reliant on the communications industry to provide the network and communication services, we also recognize that we, as an industry, are reliant on those other industries. We require industries such as electricity and gas, banking and finance, health, and government, to also function securely and without disruption to ensure the integrity of our communications infrastructure.

As recognized by the Department of Homeland Security, the Nation is dependent on the critical infrastructure of communications, banking and finance, power, food, health, information technology and others. A disruption to any component affects the whole infrastructure. Securing against disruptions to any component is in the best interest of all.

**In what areas are current cyber security technical solutions for the communications sector inadequate? Where is further research needed to mitigate existing and emerging threats and vulnerabilities?**

The communications industry is also increasingly dependent on application and information technology vendors to ensure the products they provide are of the highest quality and integrity. Software and hardware that does not meet industry security best practices and standards require additional efforts and expense to meet its expected function. Vendors that provide software or hardware with security vulnerabilities that must constantly be monitored, reviewed, and patched, are a drain on a company's resources and a liability to companies that must ensure the integrity of their systems, data, and services.

SBC works diligently with software vendors that provide the foundation of the information technology infrastructure to ensure necessary software security patches are installed to protect our complex environment. Continued focus from the Federal Government on industry standards for secure information technology products is appreciated and desired. This will help to ensure that better security and quality is an objective of the software, network and computer hardware industries.

NIST (National Institute of Standards and Technology) is one example of a collaborative organization that has been helpful in promoting information security requirements through its various research and standards efforts. We, as a business, look to leverage those standards as potential baselines in our efforts and are glad to see vendors meet such useful guidelines.

**How should federal agencies, such as DHS, the National Science Foundation, the National Institute of Standards and Technology, and the Defense Advanced Research Projects Agency, and the academic researchers work with industry to define priorities for and support research in these areas?**

Cyber security must become a priority in the creation of new information technologies. To date, security components for information technologies often appeared to be an afterthought. Examples of this can be seen in early versions of cellular and Wi-Fi technologies, where calls could be intercepted, cell phones cloned, and data snooping could occur.

Internet Protocol (IP) based services wrestle constantly with the need to traverse the same network paths where unscrupulous persons may have the ability to interfere, impede, or intrude on the service itself. IP based services must find new ways to protect the content of each packet that is carried and delivered in this shared Internet world.

We have all seen that virus and worm attacks have risen over the past several years. Research focus on how to prevent the distribution of malicious content through virus, worms, and e-mail should be a high priority for all industries that use the Internet for communications and business. The ability to detect and remove unwanted data content and attacks as it progresses through the network is more desirable than expecting each end device to have the same ability to protect itself from its neighbors on the networks.

Admittedly, security requirements interfere with convenience of the product or service offered. However, we need cyber security and software development standards that insist new technologies embrace security as part of their evolution and development. In this way, society as a whole benefits through improved assurance of integrity, reliability, service, and subsequent reduced resource costs to support those services.

SBC is committed to work with the information industry to build the next generation of Internet-based voice, video and data communications, securely.

**What are the most critical responsibilities of the Department of Homeland Security (DHS) in cyber security for the communications sector and what are the most urgent steps the new Assistant Secretary for Cyber Security and Telecommunications should take?**

Mr. Chairman and Members of the Committee, your assistance to focus industry attention on cyber security is greatly appreciated. We encourage the Department of Homeland Security to continue:

- to support research grants and assistance that focus on National cyber security,
- to support industry organizations and government agencies that create security standards and best practices,
- to continue to provide early warnings of security events, through various government agencies,
- and to make sure the security best practices that various critical government agencies develop are shared with our critical infrastructure industries.

I would like to add that you should make sure our laws carry serious penalties for cyber security issues and that the instigators are prosecuted to the full extent of the law. It must become a major crime. It is no longer just kids playing with computers. The attacks are serious.

Thank you for the opportunity to appear before you today. The work you are doing is critical to our future as a nation. Cyber terrorism is a real threat and we must stay diligent.

### Biography for Andrew M. Geisse

Andy Geisse, Chief Information Officer, is responsible for Information Technology, Payroll and Billing Operations for SBC Communications, Inc. and its subsidiaries. He was appointed to this position in October 2004 and is located in San Antonio, Texas.

Andy began his telecommunications career in 1979 with Southwestern Bell Telephone Company as Assistant Manager for the comptrollers department. He then held a variety of information technology, sales, and strategic marketing positions for Southwestern Bell and SBC Communications Inc. Andy served as Executive Director, Wireless Product Development for Southwestern Bell Mobile Systems and Vice President and General Manager for Southwestern Bell Mobile Systems' Oklahoma and West Texas regions.

In 1995, he moved to Santiago, Chile, and served as Vice President and Chief Executive Officer of VTR Cellular. He later became President of the Board of STARTEL Communications, the first nationwide cellular company in Chile. SBC had interests in both companies.

In January 1998, Andy moved to New York, as President and General Manager of SBC's Cellular One upstate New York subsidiary. Later that year, he became Vice President Enterprise and OSS Systems for SBC and its subsidiaries, located in San Ramon, California. In October 1999 Andy was appointed Senior Vice President, Enterprise Software Solutions, responsible for corporate-wide software solutions.

Andy grew up in Minneapolis, Minnesota, and St. Louis, Missouri. He earned a Bachelor's degree in Economics and Mathematics from the University of Missouri-Columbia and a M.B.A. from Washington University in St. Louis. He and his wife, Jane, have four children.

SBC

Andy Geisse
Chief Information Officer

SBC Communications Inc.
175 E. Houston
Room 1252
San Antonio, TX 78205

210-351-5120 Phone
210-351-3661 Fax

September 13, 2005

The Honorable Sherwood Boehlert
Chairman
Committee on Science
U.S. House of Representatives
2320 Rayburn House Office Building
Washington, DC 20515

Dear Congressman Boehlert:

Thank you for the invitation to testify before the Committee on Science of the U.S. House of Representatives on September 15th for the hearing entitled "*Cybersecurity: How Can the Government Help Address Vulnerabilities in Critical Industries?*" In accordance with the Rules Governing Testimony, this letter serves as formal notice of the federal funding SBC Communications Inc. ("SBC") currently receives related to the hearing topic.

Specifically, SBC has received no federal funding directly supporting the subject matter on which I will testify in the current fiscal year or either of the two proceeding fiscal years.

Sincerely,

DISCUSSION

Chairman BOEHLERT. Thank you very much, and thank all of you.

You know, one of the dangers of a hearing dealing with a sensitive subject like this is that we provide fire for tabloid trash. And I darn sure don't want to go to my supermarket checkout counter next week, and I do the grocery shopping incidentally, and read a headline that says, you know, "Science Committee Warns Cyber Katrina Imminent."

Now having said that, and taking that risk, using DHS's own color-coding system, I would say the threat is, at a minimum, at best, yellow, and perhaps even orange.

My question to all of you is do you think collectively, one, the private sector gets it and understands the full dimensions and implications, and two, the government understands the full dimensions and potential implications?

Let me ask each of you. Mr. Geisse?

Mr. GEISSE. Yes, Chairman Boehlert.

I believe the private sector understands it is critical, and I also do believe the government does as well.

But I think it is sometimes an afterthought in the sense that it is more of a technology issue and it is not only a technology issue. It is truly a part of our critical infrastructure and something that we have to be focused on as a country.

Chairman BOEHLERT. Mr. Freese.

Mr. FREESE. I think both the government and the private sector understand the issues. I see some basic fundamental problems, though, in addressing these issues as a combined force. Just as I referred to in my comments, information sharing with DHS has got to be extremely frustrating for them. They ask for information on critical infrastructure assets. We can't provide that, because there is no way that they can protect that information. It stalls the whole process.

Chairman BOEHLERT. So it is very necessary for the government and the private sector to cooperate, but you don't have the confidence——

Mr. FREESE. Absolutely.

Chairman BOEHLERT.—that the information you share, and that is very important information to determine vulnerability and response capability. You are concerned about providing that, because you are concerned about the security of sharing proprietary information—all right.

Mr. FREESE. That is correct, Mr. Chairman.

And that has been going on for a couple of years now.

Chairman BOEHLERT. Well, we are going to change it.

Mr. Kepler.

Mr. KEPLER. Yes, I think industry has put the time into this thing and understands the risks-based approach. The concern I would have is that there is a lot of problems in cyber security and are we focused on getting the right solutions for the major issues so at the end you can work on everything and not be effective in anything. And I think we really have to be focused on the major, national impacts as a first wave of fixing things.

Chairman BOEHLERT. Mr. Leggate.

Mr. LEGGATE. I would say, in my experience, that most boards get it. Most boards who run serious companies understand their dependency, in this age, on this whole digital environment. So that, I think, is done.

Whether small businesses understand the services that they need for everyday transactions, I am not sure about that.

On the government level, I would say in the United States, maybe—who understand entirely departmentally the issue. Where the challenge comes, I think, is to put this into practical action in a timely way and to then set a set of priorities become of—almost a national plan to do things very quickly in a focused way, not across a whole landscape, but just nail the big issues. And to me, that is where the gap is.

Chairman BOEHLERT. Yes. And let me ask, and one of the lessons learned from Katrina is diffused responsibility. Everybody's responsibility tends to be no one's responsibility. Where would you suggest the focal point should be? I am encouraged, as I hope you are, that the Secretary has announced the creation of an Assistant Secretary for Cyber Security and Telecommunications. Would that be the focal point? I mean, there is somebody that has to be sort of at the center of coordinating all of these activities. You can't have 14 people the center of coordination, because they don't coordinate amongst themselves.

Where would you suggest that be?

Mr. Leggate.

Mr. LEGGATE. Well, I would separate the notion of coordination from accountability. So coordination is a fine thing to do, and done well is good. But where do we look for the ultimate accountability for the service level we get from the Internet? To whom do we look of that? And so I think big steps to go forward to improve coordination, but I do think at some level we must actually break through into accountabilities that isn't visible today.

Chairman BOEHLERT. Mr. Kepler.

Mr. KEPLER. Yes. I think information technology is pervasive, so the idea that you would have a focused effort on cyber security, we think, is exactly correct. But to John Leggate's point is that when you think about emergency response, you think about physical securing of critical infrastructure. Those also have Internet impacts. So the—you can't separate all of these things in the Departments and have them link together. You have to have coordination but then recognition that these bodies really have to work together to come with—come up with common capabilities to, you know, defend, protect, and respond.

Chairman BOEHLERT. Mr. Freese.

Mr. FREESE. I agree. I think the coordination, I think, should lie at that new position's role. But again, and I may sound like a broken record here, but if there is going to be a coordination point, there has to be representation, and strong representation, from the private sector to assist in that coordination, because I have seen too many times in the past, it looks like a good thing to do from an overall perspective, but it is not focused to where it really needs to be.

Chairman BOEHLERT. Mr. Geisse.

Mr. GEISSE. Well, I think you brought up a good point, Mr. Chairman. I think we have lots of agencies focused on cyber security, but we don't have a single, real focal point. And maybe by the Department of Homeland Security setting this up, it should help do that.

Chairman BOEHLERT. So I would take it that your reaction is the same as mine: the welcoming of the announcement by the Secretary that we are going to have a new Assistant Secretary for Cyber Security and Telecommunications, the sooner the better.

Mr. GEISSE. Yes, sir.

Chairman BOEHLERT. But that is progress. We are moving in the right direction.

The red light is on for me. And I have got to practice what I preach, so I have got to shut up and now recognize Mr. Gordon.

Mr. GORDON. Thank you, Mr. Chairman.

And because we do have that red light, in all due respect, I would like for you to try to be crisp in your answers. And let me tell you, I want to ask each of our industry sector representatives to tell me what they think about how vulnerable your sector might be to a serious, focused, cyber attack; what could be the consequences of that attack for your industry; and what role would you suggest for Homeland Security or other parts of the Federal Government in trying to help you develop a plan and also more preferably, avoid that, and then if there is something that happens, the recovery?

And while you are thinking about that, let me quickly ask a question for Mr. Purdy.

Mr. Purdy, I recognize you are just recently been appointed the Acting Director of the agency, and so all of the either omissions or, probably more likely, the low priority that the agency has placed toward cyber security over the last four years can't be laid at your feet. But it seems like your testimony mostly was a litany of things you want to do or you are starting to do and that, really, the only plans are really just a framework document. This is concurred by the General Accounting Office, which had a report this summer that said the DHS has not yet developed national cyber threat and vulnerability assessments or government industry contingency recovery plans for cyber security. And so my really simple question is, when do you estimate these assessments and recovery plans will be in place?

Mr. PURDY. Well, attempting to comply with your request that we be succinct, let me say that I am proud to associate myself with the activity of the Department of Homeland Security since it was set up. I worked on the National Strategy to Secure Cyberspace on the White House staff and then came over to the Department to help set up this agency, and I have been Acting Director since October of last year.

We have made tremendous progress in building our watching warning capability——

Mr. GORDON. Yes, and I don't mean to be disrespectful, but I said one simple question. When do you estimate that these assessments and recovery plans will be in place?

Mr. PURDY. We have a couple different levels. The fundamental response to attacks is the ESF–2, is the communications piece, which is we have a close partnership with NCS and NCSD, that is in place. It is operational. There is a long history of the communications——

Mr. GORDON. Was it in place when the General Accounting Office did their report this summer?

Mr. PURDY. Yes, it was.

Mr. GORDON. Well, they didn't seem to think it was in place.

Mr. PURDY. Well, reading the entire GAO report, there is a recognition of tremendous progress we have made——

Mr. GORDON. Recently.

Mr. PURDY.—in a number of places.

Mr. GORDON. Right. Recently.

Mr. PURDY. And the ESF–2 is a long-standing product of a public/private partnership with the private sector that has stood the test of time, and we are proud to be associated with that. The actual assessment of risk is part of the National Infrastructure Protection Plan. The base plan will be out later this year, and each individual sector is working on developing——

Mr. GORDON. You said the base plan. That will still just be the framework?

Mr. PURDY. Yeah, the federal plan, the more detailed guidance of——

Mr. GORDON. But again, I just had a very simple question. When do you estimate these assessments and recovery plans will be in place?

Mr. PURDY. There are two different elements. There is the assessment and there is recovery.

Mr. GORDON. Okay.

Mr. PURDY. The National Infrastructure Protection Plan is part of the assessment. We are also, within the Information Analysis and Infrastructure Protection Division, doing a risk assessment of cyber that is one of the priority efforts to fuse intelligence, to map the threat against the risk. So that is going to be ready very soon. The National Infrastructure Protection Plan, the risk assessment piece, will be early next year as to when that part of the assessment is completed.

Mr. GORDON. Right. Thank you. I just didn't want to take time from these other folks.

Now, if you could, I would like to hear about your sectors.

Mr. LEGGATE. Okay. Let me speak for that.

I answer your question in—although it is a simple question, in two ways.

The first one is today, 2005, I will take a point in time in 2007 or 2008. So given we are still in the process of migration from private networks to the Internet, the consequences would be moderate in the near-term, because we haven't fully migrated to the new way. I would suggest to you that by 2007 and 2008, this is the tipping point when most the business will run that way. And at that point, I would suggest, it might be catastrophic.

Mr. GORDON. And is there a role for the United States Federal Government to play in helping you avoid catastrophe or to recover from it if it did occur?

Mr. LEGGATE. I think, absolutely, going back to the Chairman's remarks about setting up a new post within the Department, I think the issue is to make progress and retain focus to put things in place in the near time frame rather than taking five or six years to move to a better place.

Mr. KEPLER. Yes, if you take the first point, which is what I do believe is a major risk or consequence here, if communications, both voice and the Internet, is the key vulnerability in my mind and risk. If communication stops, commerce stops. And if communications isn't there, you can't recover. So really, looking at a major catastrophic failure in communications is really the real critical issue, in my mind, around cyber security. And so when you approach that, what are the major risk areas for that to happen we will have to address, and not only recover and response, but part of addressing with risk is containment and mitigation. So when we have those risks, we do see parts of the infrastructure fail, but we can't have it cascade and completely fail. So how do you contain those failures is something that we need to work on, and that needs to be collectively done between the government and industry to model those threats and to come up with response positions.

Mr. FREESE. From the electric sector, it measures very well with what he is saying. The telecommunications infrastructure and the electric infrastructure are very closely matched. A problem with telecommunications will impact the electric control systems, in most cases. If I look at it strictly from an electric company—or electric sector perspective, we are vulnerable to an undetermined extent based on the number of utilities that are in the country and the number—the amount of information that is shared even between utilities is very scarce. I can say if we have network security in place, if we have our communications security in place, we are all right. But I don't know how many of the companies are in that situation. I would say the government can assist with that by, as I mentioned, keeping the R&D programs with the Idaho National Lab, Pacific Northwest National Lab, Sandia in place, and working on cyber solutions that we need now. I mean, research and development for long-term solutions is great, but we have some pressing issues now.

Mr. GEISSE. I guess I would add, for the communications industry, it is very similar to the other industries with one exception. We keep our network, general purpose type network for our customers, independent and separate of the Internet network to try to prevent that sort of issue to begin with.

And I think you also asked what do we do about it if that happens, we have a very focused effort, something that we constantly test and for disaster recovery. If we have a disaster like that, how do we bring up a duplicate, for example, network operations center. We have duplication throughout our network to prevent it.

I think the government can help in a lot of ways. One is hearings like this that put some focus on it are important. I think doing R&D and research is important. But I also think, from my own perspective, there are reasons for these attacks, and you need to start treating them just like you are treating terrorists and other things and actually go after them and prevent it before it happens.

Mr. GORDON. Thank you very much.

Chairman BOEHLERT. Thank you very much.

The gentleman's time has expired.

And before I turn to the eloquent Mr. Akin, just let me point out the private sector. All of your affiliations have active lobbying efforts on Capitol Hill. And my experience with lobbyists; they are very valuable assets. They provide additional information to us, and hopefully we listen to both sides of the story, but that you have got to attach a higher priority to lobbying the Congress, our colleagues outside this committee, who don't really understand the full dimensions of this yet to, when you call on the Members, advocate for more R&D, for example, into cyber security, for better coordination, for more attention.

And so please carry that back to your hired guns, so to speak. And I use that as a positive not a pejorative. But you have got to focus on the importance of this subject. And tomorrow's papers will come out. The evening news will come out. Then this won't even be mentioned anyplace, because, as I say, in most quarters it is greeted with a muffled yawn, and yet we know, you know in your sharing with us, how important this is and the potential impact it could have on our entire economy.

So with that, let me turn to the always eloquent Mr. Akin.

Mr. AKIN. Thank you, Mr. Chairman.

I will try not to be too long in my eloquence here. I just had a couple of quick questions.

And let me explain where I am coming from. I am also serving on the Armed Services Committee, and one of the things that the House is doing is trying to do a complete analysis of where we are relative to defense and all. So my questions are more directed toward a situation where somebody, even a major nation state, might try to precipitate some coordinated attack in this area.

So my first question is kind of a simple one. After September 11, cell phones and phones became pretty much inoperative. Was that because of the volume of traffic?

Mr. GEISSE. I guess I will answer that one, Congressman Akin. Are you talking about specifically in New York?

Mr. AKIN. Well, actually, here in DC, cell phones were useless. You couldn't get a call or anything.

Mr. GEISSE. I am not familiar with that, but my guess I mean, the reality is of how those networks are designed, there is a limited amount of frequency that you get from the Federal Government for those networks, and as a result, a limited number of calls you can do at any one time. And I imagine the call volumes were way high that day.

Mr. AKIN. So consequently, that would jam everything up?

Mr. GEISSE. Well, I am sure there is a certain amount of calls that would get through. But one of the things that we do that you may not be aware of is for the Federal Government, in an emergency like that, we reserve a certain amount of the network for them, from a priority perspective for calls.

Mr. AKIN. Okay. Now let us say that we are talking about more this organized sort of attack type of situation. First of all, just simply how vulnerable are we? And second of all, what are some of the first things that you would do to try to protect against that?

Mr. GEISSE. As part of the co-chairs of the National Cyber Response Coordination Group in Department of Defense, and their representatives include those from the Office of the Secretary and the Joint Task Force on Global Network Operations, we have been doing tabletop exercises among the membership at the National Defense University to make sure we have the communication paths and processes in place to make sure we have a coordinated government response to such attacks.

Mr. AKIN. Anybody else want to take a shot at that?

Mr. KEPLER. I would just say that when you get prepared for the scenario you are talking about, you have to worry about diversity before you start, so we would look at cell phones, land lines, priority lines, multiple carriers, Internet communications, so the whole concept, I think in this environment, is diversity so you can respond over whatever happens to be up at the time. That is the key point in my mind.

Mr. AKIN. So you are saying have enough backup kinds of systems that are going different ways that you could run things a different direction?

Mr. KEPLER. It is hard in scenario planning to target an exact backup. That is why I think diversification of different types of routing, circuitry, different methods, whether that is satellite or whatever, are pretty key, because then you would have to take out different types of infrastructure, which is a challenge.

Mr. GEISSE. I would like to add one thing, Congressman Akin. I know of at least one situation that is public, it was in the private sector, where a cyber attack was used specifically to gather information from a competitor, so they put out a virus that basically the company didn't even know was there, collected data, transmitted it back. And so I think that type of attack that you bring up is very possible, and I think part of it is we have to start getting proactive. We can't keep sitting back and preventing after we see the worm, after we see the virus. We have to start getting and creating technologies that go out and prevent it before it ever happens.

Mr. AKIN. Right. So now some of what we have got is going to be software-related types of attacks. Some are going to be just simple hardware things like, you know, an electromagnetic pulse or something that is just simply blowing up a communications hub or something, right? And so what you are saying is a diversity of ways of moving information is probably your best—and you are saying that we are making some progress in that regard or that we still have—what is your—what would you say would be our level of vulnerability? Could you just hit the system in a couple of places and shut the country down or would it be pretty hard to just pick several things to do?

Mr. FREESE. From the communications perspective, as it applies to electricity, you could shut down various areas and regions. I don't think you could shut down the entire country. That is a—that is kind of a misconception. You could take out a significant region of power and communications, however.

Mr. AKIN. From an electric grid point of view?

Mr. FREESE. From an electric and a communications point of view.

Mr. AKIN. Yeah.

Mr. FREESE. I don't think you would have an entire country down from a telecommunications perspective from a localized attack against a certain region.

Mr. AKIN. Again——

Mr. GORDON. Would the gentleman yield? Ask him how long. He is going to be down for how long?

Mr. AKIN. Go ahead. Yeah.

Mr. GORDON. If you would. I mean, you say we would be down, but for what period of time?

Mr. FREESE. Well, that depends on a lot of different things. It depends on what you have for backup communications.

Mr. GORDON. Are we talking minutes, hours, or days, or weeks?

Mr. FREESE. I would say, in some cases, hours, some cases, days. He would be better to tell you how long it would take telecommunications to come back up.

Mr. AKIN. Yes. You can go ahead and respond.

Mr. GORDON. Thank you.

Mr. GEISSE. Yes, sir.

From a communications perspective on a cyber attack, the way we do our networks, it wouldn't affect the communications network itself, because we keep it independent. But what it does impact is the systems we use to monitor it, to provision it, to make sure that we can keep the network up. And that is why it is still extremely critical. And I think that Mr. Leggate made a point earlier on that as the future goes on, and more and more things run on the Internet itself, we more and more vulnerable versus the separate networks that we have today.

Mr. AKIN. So to some degree, the lack of sophistication, if you will, or the duplication, is giving us a lot more protection than we would have in the future? That is a point several of you have made then.

Yes. Well, I think my time has expired, and I don't want to be excessively eloquent, so——

Chairman BOEHLERT. Well, all right. Fine. We will permit you to be excessively eloquent.

But Mr. Purdy, you had your hand up.

Mr. PURDY. Yes. I just wanted to mention that in a major situation, we have the critical infrastructure warning information network that is a survivable network connecting our Department with various critical sectors in the country, including electricity, information technology, and telecommunications, State Homeland Security Advisors, sector-specific agencies, and resources in each critical infrastructure, and we are building out that network to greater connectivity over time.

Chairman BOEHLERT. When the warning is issued, hopefully the message is not only heard but heeded. I would point out that one of the agencies under the jurisdiction of this committee is NOAA, which is the parent agency for the National Weather Service, and if you are looking for bright lights in the aftermath of Katrina, one of the bright lights is that the National Weather Service, on five o'clock, on the Friday preceding the Monday morning when Katrina actually hit land, the National Weather Service put out an alert, a weather alert that a category four or five hurricane was due to hit within 72 hours. That went to every emergency responder, every state capitol, every major city, but some people didn't pay much attention.

Mr. Honda.

Mr. HONDA. Thank you, Mr. Chairman, and I appreciate this opportunity.

There are two arenas I would like to just bring up, and it has been touched upon a little bit. But one is, I represent Silicon Valley, and in our valley, we house the backup data and even the primary data of many businesses. Perhaps some of yours are housed there. And maintaining both the integrity of and the appropriate access to this data is essential for normal operations. But in the event of not only a cyber attack, you have made some comments in that arena and physical attack, but coupled physical and cyber. I am not sure that that was discussed very fully. And also a response on how we would be responding to a natural disaster. And I bring that up, because my valley is situated between the San Andreas Fault and the Hayward Fault. And I am not sure that that kind of an incident or occurrence has been thought of. And given Katrina, I think that natural disasters we found that sometimes it creates a lot of unintended consequences that we have to anticipate.

The other question is the information sharing and exchange, that has always been something I have been concerned about since 9/11. And in terms of cyber security and information exchange, where are we in the Department of Homeland Security in that effort? And I would like to know what the private sector feels that we are, and what grade would you give the Department of Homeland Security at this point in time? And then I suspect that we are going to have a new Assistant Secretary of Cyber Security. What advice would you give that person at this point in time relative to information sharing?

Thank you, Mr. Chairman.

Mr. KEPLER. Let me try to answer maybe a couple from my view.

The one point you made, if you think of weather systems, we are getting a lot better at modeling hurricanes. If you think of earthquakes, we are getting better, but not nearly to the sophistication. To other external threats, we don't have the same type of modeling and predictive capabilities. So part of the response is getting that predictive capability. So we really need to think about that as we go forward and look at strengthening that. That is one of my——

Mr. HONDA. Does our—do we have a redundant system that will accommodate all of those three areas?

Mr. KEPLER. Well, there are just a couple of areas we are talking about. One is the prediction so you can become better prepared in stages. You go closer like you would. Another activity is to have diversification of your infrastructure and recovery protocols, so most major companies are positioned to have recovery plans, crisis management plans in place. We have corporate crisis management plans since the late '80s. When 9/11 occurred, we actually invoked that. We weren't majorly impacted, to one of the other points earlier, some of the small businesses and structures that may not have that level of sophistication.

I think it is also a challenge in terms of information sharing, which is critical in protecting and responding. The private sector is bound between antitrust laws and Freedom of Information issues and sharing information. That, to me, is a critical issue that we still need to balance on. So while you are trying to address this thing, we can actually be non-compliant with other laws. So how we really focus on that information sharing is really a critical aspect of it.

Mr. HONDA. Thank you.

Mr. FREESE. I would like to add something about the natural disasters response you were talking about.

Even during Katrina, there was some extensive physical damage to the electric infrastructure, to the communications infrastructure, and several others. Okay. And that is going to happen regardless of what type of natural disaster you have got. So what your main concern is, at that point, is making sure that those problems don't cascade outside of the immediately affected area. And I think it was true testimony to everybody's professionalism down there that the electric sector maintained power around the area. There were no cascading failures. Communications was set up via the Internet and temporary communications, so there are ways to do this. But I don't see a really good way around the physical damage, physical destruction of the infrastructure. That is very difficult to have a backup to outside of the affected area.

Mr. HONDA. And in the affected area, was there a replacement system that took place of the current power, no pun intended, not electrical power, because people were afraid——

Mr. FREESE. No.

Mr. HONDA.—of electrocution?

Mr. FREESE. No, there was not. There were substations that were damaged and put out of service. There were lines down. That type of physical damage just takes time to repair. Now there are ways of bringing temporary transformers in, those types of—getting the lines back up, temporary lines run, but that, of course, takes time and effort and significant funding.

Mr. HONDA. Would wireless and satellite connections replace that loss of——

Mr. FREESE. From the communications perspective, yes.

Mr. GEISSE. Yes. For example, in Hurricane Katrina, one of the first things we did is send down—we call them "cellular on wheels." They are basically cell sites that are built into a truck. We sent over 300 of those down there immediately for—so that we could set up cellular service in Katrina.

Mr. HONDA. Was that private sector strategy or was that something——

Mr. GEISSE. Private sector strategy.

Mr. HONDA. And is that something that we should look at in terms of the government's side?

Mr. GEISSE. Well, I guess here is my answer because I think your question is, as I understand, and it is well founded. I mean, you know, we have had many disasters in California from the fires down in LA to the mudslides to our own issues with flooding and weather. And we have response units within our company to go out and handle those types of situations so that we can get service up and repaired as quickly as possible. And it is not as simple as just dropping in a second system, because really, in many cases, like, for example, the fires down there, we had burned up wires that we had to go in and replace and put up and running and working. I think what the government can help on this, and I think it has been brought up here several times, is start focusing this as a major issue and that we are all prepared, as different industries, to work together in a real disaster.

Mr. FREESE. If I may just finish up with one thing about the information exchange in DHS. As I mentioned earlier, that has been a problem for the last few years, and I am not sure that I understand exactly why, because DHS has a PCII program developed and in place. This was essentially going to let private industry present information to the government that would be protected and would not be disclosed without the private industry's permission. I am not sure where that stands right now. If Mr. Purdy could give me an update on that program, I would appreciate it.

Chairman BOEHLERT. Mr. Purdy, and then we will go. Mr. Honda's time is expired. We are generous.

Mr. PURDY. Yes, the PCII program, which has been operating under an interim rule since the time it went into effect, will be subject to a final rule. It is under current consideration by the DHS General Counsel, Phil Perry. We expect that revised rule to come out momentarily. But in the meantime, we are trying to facilitate information sharing, building on some key legacy organizations, such as the NCC ISACs, the NCC generally, but we have leveraged the source of information across the federal agencies, so we get better information now, and now we can share it. Plus, we have enhanced the information we get from the intelligence and the law enforcement folks, and we can put out targeted bulletins to the technical or non-technical sector, to government or the private sector, that we don't associate with the source of the information. So we can get sensitive law enforcement-sensitive information, classified information that we can turn into actionable guidance. In addition, we are building a North American Incident Response Group of private sector folks. We met last week in Silicon Valley with a number of companies out there. We have a meeting that is ongoing right now in Arlington with a number of companies. We are trying to build that capability. The ISACs, we met with the ISAC council with the Assistant Secretary earlier this week. The sharing of information with the ISACs is a fundamentally important thing.

In addition, there has been a robust sharing among ISACs that is centered by the IT ISAC. We have our US–CERT secure portal that has 2,000 private and governmental folks involved in sharing information in a secure environment. We are going to tie in that IT ISAC information sharing, because we believe it is a combination of building trust, giving value, because we have a major private sector retreat next week that the private sector is hosting. We want to share what we know, what of that do they want, and let us accelerate the mechanisms for getting that information. Because folks, if they go to the effort or decide whether to go to the effort to share information, it is important to protect it, but it is also important for them to think somebody cares about it, somebody uses it, and we provide value back to the private sector. And we are committed to do that.

Chairman BOEHLERT. Thank you very much, Mr. Purdy.

The Chair recognizes Dr. Bartlett.

Mr. BARTLETT. Thank you very much.

Mr. Leggate, in your written testimony, you note that businesses and governments can plan for expected failures. But even the best prepared organizations and corporations may be woefully inadequate in responding to complex, low-probability, high-impact failures. If a large-scale Internet outage or significant reduction in performance would occur, the unexpected effects on whole sets of industries, utilities, and enterprise could have surprisingly large economic and social impacts. For the few moments that we have, I would like to engage you in a discussion of the ultimate low-probability, high-impact failure, and that is a nuclear EMP attack on our country.

For several years, I have been concerned with this, and I got legislation about three years ago to set up an EMP Commission which acted for two years, chaired by Dr. Bill Graham, Rumsfeld's deputy in his emerging ballistic missile threat commission. They have now issued their report. Senator John Kyl has, in the last few weeks, had a piece in the *Washington Post* reflecting his concern for this. Newt Gingrich and his colleague, Bill Forstchen, have written a fascinating novel, which will be out next summer. I encourage you to read that. It is called "One Second After." They have done very good research. It is quite accurate. Because even the level of concern may be classified, I will only tell you that within the Pentagon now, there is a growing concern for a nuclear EMP attack.

The Russian generals can tell us things that I maybe cannot tell you, because they would be classified, but the Russian generals tell us that they have developed a nuclear EMP weapon that will produce 200 kilovolts per meter, that a large weapon detonated 300 miles high over the center of our country, Iowa or Nebraska, would blanket the whole country, and at its margins, would be 100 kilovolts per meter. The Russian generals tell us that the 200 kilovolts per meter is several times the level to which we tested. I cannot tell you to which we tested. I think that is classified, but the Russian generals say that that is several times the level to which we tested. And at the margins, it is probably a couple of times to the level at which we tested.

My question is what are we doing to prepare for an EMP attack? The Commission, by the way, noted that this is one of a few incidents that could, you know, and I am going to put their caution in the common vernacular, it could end life as we know it. What preparations are we making for this low-probability, high-impact probability?

And I would like to ask Mr. Freese, if a failure of the power systems resulted in the loss of our major transformers, how long would it take to get a new one, and where would you go to get a new one?

Mr. FREESE. Okay. We have multiple sizes of transformers. Some of them are readily available in spare parts.

Mr. BARTLETT. But isn't it true, sir, that the larger ones that we don't even make in this country——

Mr. FREESE. Yes, sir. I——

Mr. BARTLETT.—it would take you maybe 18 months to get one——

Mr. FREESE. Yes, sir.

Mr. BARTLETT.—ordered from overseas?

Mr. FREESE. I was going to mention that at the——

Mr. BARTLETT. That is correct?

Mr. FREESE. There are some major transformers that are not made in this country, made in Europe and in Asia, and it would take up to 18 months to get one sent over to the United States. That is one at costs of several million dollars. And we, frankly, don't have a lot of those spare parts laying around.

Mr. BARTLETT. But you do have a few spare transformers?

Mr. FREESE. Yes.

Mr. BARTLETT. They are in the field?

Mr. FREESE. Yes.

Mr. BARTLETT. They are beside the transformer that if it went out, you couldn't serve your customers. But an EMP attack would take out both of them, would it not?

Mr. FREESE. Yes, sir, it would.

Mr. BARTLETT. I hope that my colleague, Dr. Ehlers, has an opportunity to pursue this, because already our yellow light is on.

But I want to ask each of you the level of concern in your discipline about EMP attack and what you are doing.

Let me start with Mr. Purdy. What is your level of concern, sir, and what are you doing about it?

Mr. PURDY. Well, this issue is concerned in the larger context of the full potential threats to the telecommunications infrastructure. The Department of Homeland Security is working with the Department of Defense and Central Intelligence Agency to ongoing assess the developments of the kinds of technology you are talking about to consider the full range of these kinds of threats against various sectors, including the use of EMP and telecommunications electromagnetic disruptive effects.

Mr. BARTLETT. Sir, when will you, because our time is very short, when will you be able to tell us of our level of vulnerability and your recommendations for what we do about it? Just tell us when you will be able to tell us that.

Mr. PURDY. Well, we already made recommendations and mitigative measures have been taken to enhance the equipment providing greater protection in the event of an EMP threat.

Mr. BARTLETT. My red light is on. Let me just make one observation and ask if this is not correct.

We have SCADA systems and we have computers embedded in those, and it is my understanding that we may not even know who made those computers. And if we know, they may no longer be available, there are so many of those that it would be impossible to harden them, and that unless we are going to replace all of those SCADA systems, we are going to remain vulnerable to a pretty broad scale shutdown of our infrastructure in the event of an EMP attack. That is correct?

Mr. FREESE. Well, sir, I mentioned it earlier that our electric infrastructure is made up of a lot of legacy systems that don't support new technological security protections and it will take, probably, a new generation of infrastructure to completely eradicate those from the system. Right now, we are working with obsolete equipment in a lot of cases.

Mr. BARTLETT. I know my red light is on, Mr. Chairman. I just want to note that although not one in 100 of our citizens may know about nuclear EMP attack, I will assure you, sir, that every one of our potential enemies knows all about it, and it is in their open literature.

Thank you very much.

Mr. AKIN. [Presiding] Thank you, Mr. Bartlett.

Mr. Miller.

Mr. MILLER. Thank you, Mr. Chairman.

The 9/11 Commission said that private sector preparedness for terrorism attack now must be regarded as part of the cost of doing business, certainly for critical industries and any kind of critical infrastructure. And you can no longer—no industry that is part of our critical infrastructure can ever claim again that a nuclear—that a, excuse me, terrorist attack is not foreseeable. It must be foreseeable. Do all of you agree with that?

Yes, sir.

Mr. LEGGATE. I would say the point you come to is the range of scenarios that companies use to do their testing of their systems that, in a sense, prior to 9/11, we wouldn't have conceived——

Mr. MILLER. Right.

Mr. LEGGATE.—events of this kind. But what we have to do is learn from 9/11, learn from the tsunami——

Mr. MILLER. Right.

Mr. LEGGATE.—New Orleans, and also from the bombing in London, for example, which we have been involved in managing. So each one creates a new set of situations, and then companies, and I would make a plug for this, really have to really run these scenarios hard and find out, I would call it the disconnected pieces, the things that you wouldn't have predicted that show up. And it also applies at the national level as well. So there is enormous value in running these scenarios. Then to find out the things that do fail well ahead of time.

And number two, prepare your management teams, either at the country level or the corporate level, to respond effectively during difficult situations.

Mr. MILLER. Okay. Yes, I agree with you. You can't just respond to the things that have already happened. Be prepared for things that we know can happen, because they have happened. We really do need smart people lying awake at three o'clock in the morning trying to figure out what could happen next and how to be prepared for that.

The 9/11 Commission also said that we needed to develop standards for preparedness in the private sector that does provide for business continuity and mitigation, redundancy, and that those kind of commonly understood standards, they praised the standards developed by the American National Standards Institute, ANSI, should become the standard of care for purposes of legal liability. Is there anything like that in the cyber field? Is there any kind of standard of care that is the industry standard that is well understood this is what you do to be prepared against a cyber attack?

Yes, sir.

Mr. FREESE. Yes, sir. In the electric sector, we have the North American Electric Reliability Council, twelve hundred cyber security standards. These have been in place for almost two years, and they provide a very, very solid best practices approach to securing critical security systems and other critical systems against cyber attack. It extends into business continuity, disaster recovery, personnel issues, background checks, network security, transmission security, and communications security. So these are in place right now.

Mr. MILLER. Okay. And Mr. Purdy, does the Homeland Security Department embrace the finding of the 9/11 Commission that there should be legal liability for the failure to prepare up to the standard of care in industry?

Mr. PURDY. We have not taken a position on whether there should be liability in that instance. What we are finding is that the interpretation of the Sarbanes-Oxley statute, requiring that the CEOs and Boards of Directors exercise due care in their risk mitigation processes has led the CEOs to fashion their risk mitigation strategies based on best practices. NIST provides very substantial guidance on best practices for information systems. The FISMA standards for federal systems provides similar guidance, and we are working with NIST on additional guidance along those areas.

Mr. MILLER. Okay. The usual legal liability is for the damages that would be foreseeable from a failure to abide by the legal standard of care. Mr. Freese, for instance, in the energy area in the electric grid, what would be the foreseeable loss from a cyber terror attack that was foreseeable, should have been foreseeable, and that the failure to abide by industry standards had led to it?

Mr. FREESE. Please rephrase the question for me.

Mr. MILLER. Okay. I will admit that was a little garbled. I will try that again.

What is a foreseeable loss, not just to a power company, but from all of those who do business with it who depend upon it for their power from a cyber security attack?

Mr. FREESE. Well, it is going to be very significant. From the electric sector, it is one of the primary critical infrastructures in the country. There is virtually nothing that doesn't use electricity. Businesses, the military, everything uses electricity. If you have a major cyber attack that takes out an entire region of the country, everyone is going to be impacted within that region. I mean, there is—there are some backup generators. There are backup power supplies, but essentially, a lot of companies are going to take major losses, financial losses, if there is a major outage that lasts any period of time.

Mr. AKIN. The gentleman's time has expired.

Mrs. Biggert.

Ms. BIGGERT. Thank you, Mr. Chairman.

Mr. Kepler and Mr. Freese, you both mentioned your work with the National Laboratories on your critical infrastructure protection efforts. Could you give us a little more detail about your work with the Labs? And have they been helpful?

Mr. KEPLER. Yes, I would be happy to do that.

To link the two discussions up here, from an American Chemistry Council point of view, we have a concept called "Responsible

Care" that we expect our members to subscribe to. In that is a certain set of management practices of how you approach all aspects of stewardship in your industry, including security. And in that is embedded cyber security. With that, these are management practices, and you need to establish standards of how you do that in compliance. You don't want to subscribe to exact solutions, because this is such a dynamic area. So we have worked with organizations that have been outlined, as well as international standards organizations, and tried to build those in. For example, in plant vulnerability, assessments and design is a great example. Just the corporate management systems for how you put in place corporate governance of security, including cyber security as well.

Ms. BIGGERT. Mr. Freese.

Mr. FREESE. We have worked significantly with the Idaho National Lab and Pacific Northwest National Lab on SCADA, specifically. We are looking at encryption technologies, encryption of control signals to prevent interception or injection. We are looking at secure authentication. And this is, again, this is trying to secure the current systems we have now prior to any long-term R&D coming into fruition. There is a SCADA testbed at the Idaho National Lab that is extremely valuable. It can be used to solve a lot of problems with information security, especially if it is coordinated with the—they also have an energy infrastructure set up at Idaho National Lab that has got end-to-end—well, for an example of infrastructure for telecommunications and electricity, you can do end-to-end testing, and you don't have to bother with piece meal solutions. You can go and do an entire range of trial and error. And I think those programs are extremely valuable, and they are not made enough use of right now. And I think we should expand the use of those, particularly in the SCADA testbed. There is a lot of equipment that is used commonly by many, many companies, and those would apply particularly well to that particular test environment.

Ms. BIGGERT. Thank you.

And Mr. Purdy, you know, the Labs do have expertise in both computers and the networks and the critical infrastructure protections. To what extent is your Division working with the National Labs and the U.S. research universities?

Mr. PURDY. One of the highest priority programs for NCSD is our Control Systems Security Program. We funded it at over $11 million in 2005, and the President's budget proposes over $15 million in 2006. At the heart of that is our work with the Idaho National Lab and the partnership with the other Labs and partnership with the Department of Energy on their area of responsibility, and the Science and Technology Directorate. So that is a hugely significant area that we are working in close partnership, not only with the Labs, but the key private sector folks. We helped form, for example, the Process Control Systems Forum, which is made up of hundreds of owners and operators. In addition, NIST has an Advisory Group of owners and operators. We are working with DOE to build the network of the control systems owners and operators so that we get the shared information on attacks and failures and that we can have a continuous loop, but it has R&D aspects, incident response aspects, and there are short- and long-term benefits to this program.

Ms. BIGGERT. Thank you.

And then time for one more question to Mr. Freese again.

One aspect of cyber security is making sure that the Internet and other information networks are up and running. And isn't electricity critical to keeping the information networks, like the Internet, operational? So if so, then cyber security is critical to your core business of energy production and distribution. But your core business also is critical to the cyber security of other sectors of the economy and the Nation as a whole. Is the energy sector giving equal attention to cyber security and the protection of critical energy infrastructure? Is one more important than the other or are they the same? It seems like we have got the chicken and the egg, which is going to be——

Mr. FREESE. Yeah, it is kind of a chicken and the egg situation. But I believe sincerely that the energy sector is extremely aware of their responsibilities to the rest of the country to provide communications, the Internet, all of those things. We are—we have formed major industry groups to look at security within the industry itself across the sector, physical and cyber security, physical primarily to protect the cyber assets. And we take that very seriously. And we understand that there are these interdependencies that we are a primary part of in a lot of areas in a lot of critical infrastructure sectors.

Ms. BIGGERT. Okay. Thank you.

My time has expired.

Mr. AKIN. Ms. Johnson.

Ms. JOHNSON. Thank you very much, Mr. Chairman.

I ask unanimous consent to submit my entire statement to the record and welcome this esteemed panel. And let me apologize for having to——

Mr. AKIN. Without objection, that will be entered in the record.

Ms. JOHNSON. Thank you.

I apologize for having to dash out and come back.

And Mr. Geisse, welcome. I know two of your colleagues, John Mumford, whom I served in the Texas Senate with on the Finance Committee, and Mr. Whitacre that I have known for 20 some years. So welcome to this committee.

I have some questions that I am asking anyone to answer. And maybe you have already answered, and if you have, just tell me, and I apologize for asking again.

But what is known about the vulnerabilities of different sectors of the economy that rely on networked information systems, and to what extent can the seriousness of the threat be quantified or prioritized?

Go ahead.

Mr. PURDY. The National Infrastructure Advisory Council, a Presidential Advisory Group, made up of private sector individuals, has done an assessment of the risk and threat to the different critical infrastructure sectors and the dependency of those sectors on each other. That is not available for public dissemination. We are using that as part of our process of identifying the cyber risk assessment as part of our fusion of the intelligence vulnerability and consequences information and in our work on developing scenarios that I talked about in my testimony so that we can understand what is necessary to mitigate the possibility of those vulnerabilities being exploited, how are we going to respond to those, and how are we going to reconstitute. And we look forward to that being a strong public/private partnership.

Ms. JOHNSON. Thank you.

Anyone else?

Thank you very much.

Is the government sponsoring enough R&D in an effort to aid the public sector with cyber security?

Yes.

Mr. PURDY. Let me answer the question this way.

The Federal Government, under HSPD-7, has coordinated, under the leadership of the Office of Science and Technology Policy, the President's Science Advisor, and the Science and Technology Directorate. They will be issuing a national cyber R&D plan in the very near future which will serve the benefit of scoping out what needs to be done. They also had an interagency group to identify and track what is happening and what needs to be happening in cyber security. It is my hope that as the articulation of what needs to be done and the specific requirements are laid out, then those who feel that the priorities aren't the right priorities or feel that the resources aren't the right ones, then, perhaps, can suggest where the extra emphasis and resources need to be placed.

Ms. JOHNSON. Do I have a little bit more time for another question? I guess——

Mr. AKIN. The gentlelady does have a minute and 43 seconds.

Ms. JOHNSON. Okay. Thank you.

There are two aspects of cyber security that I have concern about, because of my constituency and because of Homeland Security. One is that I have not met a person who is not suspicious of all of their business being available through the networks. And I would like some comment on that on just how secure that is, and two, for terrorist attacks.

So I invite anyone to comment to see what we need to do or what is the risk or what is real and what is imagined.

Mr. KEPLER. On the second part, I think when you look at the access to terrorism, this is a critical issue in terms of the amount of information we want to provide in this country versus how that information could be used against us. And certainly, I mean, that is one of the public policy things that needs to be addressed. What we want to do is be able to have an open environment between the right people to make sure we can assess threat. The challenge is once you start to look at those vulnerabilities and make them public, they provide information to our enemies as well. And the challenge we have is some things that may not be related to terrorism directly can be used as information to create attacks. And I think we have to spend a lot of time on public policy and on research to figure out how to segment those two issues and keep them balanced.

Ms. JOHNSON. Are you doing any kind of PR to allay the fears of Americans who think that telephone companies and everybody else snoop into their business by computer and Internet?

Mr. GEISSE. Telephone companies snooping?

Ms. JOHNSON. Anything wired, people think they can listen to their conversations, get into their private business, look at where they shop, all of that.

Mr. GEISSE. Well, I think, you know, I will answer your question in that your concern about terrorist attack, your concern about information being available on the Internet are real issues, and they are issues that industry has to constantly be looking at to protect our customers' information, which, for example, we do in the phone company religiously. I mean, we take it very, very serious, our customer information and protecting it, and are constantly looking for ways to prevent attacks on that information.

Ms. JOHNSON. Thank you.

Would anybody else like to comment or do you think you are saved by the bell?

Mr. AKIN. The gentlelady's——

Ms. JOHNSON. My time is up.

Mr. AKIN.—time is——

Ms. JOHNSON. Thank you very much.

Mr. AKIN.—expired, and we have a vote on the House Floor, but if Dr. Ehlers can go quickly, we can get that in, I think.

Mr. EHLERS. I thank you, Mr. Chairman.

I will try to be pretty rapid.

First of all, to respond to my colleague who just asked the question about telephone companies snooping. I grew up in southwest Minnesota, a very small town, hand crank telephone on the wall, a switchboard sitting downtown with an operator, and I can tell you, she knew more about the business of everyone in the town than anyone else did. So I suspect there is considerably less snooping by telephone companies by electronics than there was back then. But it is certainly a worthwhile question to ask.

I would like to, first of all, just sitting here trying to put this all in perspective, it seems to me that most of the discussion has been about cyber security in the sense of software, and that is, of course, a major concern. It is a concern both in terms of industrial espionage, as it is called, certainly a concern in terms of national security. But then there is also the hardware factor, which was brought up by my colleague from Maryland. And since we are both scientists, maybe we have good reason for both worrying about the same thing, namely the hardware security.

We have known about nuclear EMP for a long time. And I happen to be a nuclear physicist and worked at Livermore for one summer, years ago. And I never worried that much about it, because, frankly, I thought mutually assured destruction was pretty clear policy in that there is no benefit in any country to set off a nuclear weapon far above another country knowing that they, in turn, would have their systems destroyed. I do worry about it much, much more now, and I think Dr. Bartlett's fear is well founded in the sense that if you don't have a country that can be counterattacked, and if your goal is to disable your opponent as much as possible and to cause grief and pain and terror, the EMP is a very good way to do it, if you can manage to get the weapon and the launch vehicle. And I think it is something we have to take very seriously. Mr. Freese, I think you were a little optimistic in saying it would only affect certain areas of the country, but it depends, again, on the size of the weapon. We are not hardening our equipment.

And I was struck by a phrase that Mr. Kepler offered earlier that when communication stops, commerce stops. And I would even extend that beyond that. When commerce stops, then life is endangered and perhaps life stops, because with the proliferation, and I have been worrying about this for about 10 years now. I never worried about it too much until the proliferation of the Internet, but today, so much commerce is done over the Internet. But also, the proliferation of microprocessors and automobiles and everywhere else. And an EMP would not only affect communications but also transportation. How many of us would be able to drive our car after an EMP had wiped out the processors? And there are some 250, typically, microprocessors in the average American automobile today. How would trucks be able to deliver a product? How would people get food and water? I mean, this is really a doomsday scenario.

And Mr. Purdy, I hope that you and others are worrying a great deal about this, because what we really need in place is an infrastructure that, at least in an emergency basis, would replace the infrastructure that we are becoming so dependent on through our use of microprocessors, Internet, and so forth.

And I would like to give any of you time to react to my comments. Maybe I am off base, and if so, I would like to hear that. But if you could, briefly make a comment.

Mr. Kepler.

Mr. KEPLER. Yes, Congressman.

I think one of the key issues as we talk about industry and government relationship is understanding the roles and responsibilities. It is probably not practical for companies to go address that problem. That requires government from that type of level, and that is my broader point is these major issues need to be led by government in terms of how we address in the sectors need to support. There are things the sectors need to do, but there are things the government needs to do in that environment.

Mr. EHLERS. If I may just interject. It seems to me your role, however, is to try to harden your facilities so that you can continue to operate.

Mr. KEPLER. Absolutely, and that is why we need diversification and structure. One point that has been brought up is the idea that the older technology can't be replaced, and that is true, but also the older technology is less vulnerable to the newer threats. So it is a real delicate balance in terms of putting this new technology in, because it is actually more vulnerable because of its complexity and size. So that is why I think we have got to be really careful of just putting technical solutions in and not having the broad policy understandings and risk balancing here.

Mr. EHLERS. That is precisely the point, and the policy has to come from the Federal Government, but also the industry has to be aware of the need to harden their facilities as much as they can so at least emergency services can continue.

Mr. KEPLER. We agree with that.

Mr. EHLERS. Mr. Purdy, do you have a comment?

Mr. PURDY. I will have to defer to National Communication Systems on your follow-up question.

Mr. EHLERS. Any other comments?

I think everyone is eager to go vote, and I am as popular as a skunk at the tea party at this point, so I will defer to the Chairman and yield back.

Mr. AKIN. No, you are very popular, Dr. Ehlers.

And—but your time has expired.

And now all of our time is expired, because we have got to go vote.

We will leave the record open for five days for Members to submit additional written questions for the witnesses.

And I want to thank the witnesses for your time and your testimony. You are experts in your fields, and you have added to our understanding, and we thank you.

And the Committee stands adjourned.

[Whereupon, at 12:00 p.m., the Committee was adjourned.]

# Appendix:

## Answers to Post-Hearing Questions

ANSWERS TO POST-HEARING QUESTIONS

*Responses by Donald "Andy" Purdy, Jr., Acting Director, National Cyber Security Division, Department of Homeland Security*

**Questions submitted by Chairman Sherwood L. Boehlert**

*Q1. Measuring Cyber Security*

*Q1a. How do you measure national cyber security?*

*A1a.* National cyber security is a rapidly changing area in which a dynamic market drives the continuous emergence of new technologies and an evolving threat environment. As a result, measuring national cyber security is an important but challenging goal.

Organizations, including all levels of industry, government, and academia, do not necessarily have total network cognizance, which prevents them from being able to measure their own level of security. To create an assessment of national cyber security, an entity would require accurate reporting from all organizations that rely on cyber systems on their own individual networks. Until all organizations achieve this, it will be very difficult to measure national cyber security.

NCSD is working toward achieving greater situational awareness through efforts with: federal agencies, such as federal agency network monitoring; the private sector through interaction with Information Sharing and Analysis Center (ISACs); and, international partners through the international Computer Emergency Response Team collaboration. Enhanced situational awareness will help to provide a better estimation of the state of cyber security and identify methods of measuring changes and improvement.

In addition, NCSD's responsibilities under the National Infrastructure Protection Plan (NIPP) for the IT Sector and cyber guidance across the critical infrastructures, will involve working with key governmental entities and the private sector to complete a sector specific plan that when implemented will help to create a national assessment of cyber risk, together with the prioritization of cyber risk mitigation measures. Several critical infrastructure cyber measures and metrics will be tracked across each sector based on the Sample Cyber Measures and Metrics being developed for the NIPP.

The Counter-intelligence community also supports these efforts from the perspective of cyber espionage threat assessments. Foreign intelligence services are increasingly using cyber espionage as a means for collecting sensitive information. We are developing methodologies for identifying their cyber capabilities and for assessing, in more precise form, the damage to national security that might be caused by various cyber intrusion incidents.

*Q1b. How do you determine if the Nation's level of cyber vulnerability is being reduced?*

*A1b.* In order to determine whether the Nation's level of cyber vulnerability is being reduced, NCSD undertakes a risk management approach that includes measuring threat, vulnerability, and consequences.

There are a number of DHS initiatives underway that examine cyber-related vulnerabilities in addition to physical risk and vulnerability assessments. In coordination with the private sector, DHS is identifying cyber vulnerability assessment best practices. This effort began with an evaluation of various methodologies in use throughout the public and private sectors. In addition, NCSD is working closely with other DHS components to ensure that cyber aspects of threat, consequence, and vulnerability analysis are consistently and appropriately included in risk methodology efforts. These efforts include the Risk Analysis and Management for Critical Asset Protection (RAMCAP), the Vulnerability Identification Self Assessment Tool, Comprehensive Reviews, and Site Assistance Visits.

NCSD is sponsoring several exercise initiatives that will enhance U.S. preparedness in the event of a cyber incident and improve communication, coordination, and procedures between DHS, other government agencies, the public and private sectors, and with select foreign partners. In February 2006, NCSD will conduct the National Cyber Exercise: Cyber Storm, which will test federal response to a cyber-related incident of national significance; examine state, federal and international intra-governmental coordination; and emphasize public/private cooperation and communications using the energy, information technology, telecommunications and transportation sectors. In addition to Cyber Storm, NCSD has also coordinated extensively with and supported the creation of two regional partnerships in the Gulf Coast and the Pacific Northwest consisting of public and private sector entities. In each of these regions, NCSD has facilitated a tabletop exercise designed to raise awareness of infrastructure interdependencies and to identify ways to improve regional preparedness. Collaboration with State/local government and private sector companies has been instrumental in the success of our regional efforts in the Gulf Coast and Pacific Northwest. Through direct interaction and collaboration during exercises in these regions, NCSD has developed significant partnerships with the public and private sectors to better prepare for and become more capable of preventing, responding to, and recovering from a major cyber incident.

Cyber exercises provide the environment to develop, coordinate, rehearse, and refine key processes; integrate infrastructure protection activities within other national-level plans; establish mechanisms for coordination and information exchange; and identify interdependencies, overlaps, and gaps so that all the critical infrastructure stakeholders at every level are better prepared for and more capable of preventing, responding to, and recovering from a major cyber incident, thereby reducing exposure to cyber vulnerabilities.

*Q1c. How do you decide what is "secure enough"?*

*A1c.* Determining a sufficient level of security is variable depending on the specific needs of an organization and the specific assets involved, their risk tolerance, and the availability of resources. By following established set standards such as International Organization for Standardization (ISO) 17799, an international security standard that includes a comprehensive set of controls comprising best practices in information security, as well as conducting risk assessments, entities may determine their ideal security level. This determination must be based upon the results of a risk assessment in which government and the private sector respectively, can reasonably decide what level of risk is acceptable or what areas need improvement and additional effort. Entities will make the determination regarding whether or not improvements and additional effort are necessary, based on availability of resources concerning their risk assessments and acceptable levels of risk.

*Q1d. Are government mandates needed to increase the Nation's progress on securing information systems and to get to "secure enough"?*

*A1d.* Government mandates would likely not increase the Nation's progress on securing systems to reach a state of "secure enough." This is largely due to the fact that a state of "secure enough" will differ for each entity utilizing information systems and the fact that it would be very difficult to formulate a mandate that enhances security in a way that can evolve with the dynamic security and technology environment. Each operating environment is different and each entity, public or private, must determine what is needed to continue their individual critical operations based on their distinct environment. These case-specific needs will evolve over time.

A comprehensive awareness program to include the promotion of a risk management approach, as well as accepted best practices and standards, is a more effective tool for enhancing cyber security and achieving a greater state of security. Under the NIPP framework, metrics are being developed to improve the measurement of cyber security across critical infrastructure sectors.

*Q2. Information Sharing*

*Q2a. What information would Department of Homeland Security (DHS) find most helpful to receive from critical infrastructure and information technology companies? What do you, or would you, do with this information, and how would you protect sensitive information?*

*A2a.* Industry information can allow NCSD (in partnership with other government entities and the private sector) to identify critical assets and interdependencies, vulnerabilities, and problematic cyber incidents and activity, assess cyber risk and prioritize measures to reduce vulnerabilities and cyber risk, generally, and minimize the severity of cyber attacks by timely warnings and by increased awareness and outreach efforts to improve the cyber security of critical infrastructures. DHS has established mechanisms, such as the Protected Critical Infrastructure Information program (PCII), to encourage industry to submit proprietary/sensitive information that will be protected and exempt from public disclosure as determined by the PCII program. In addition, entities may securely submit information through the United States Computer Emergency Readiness Team (US–CERT) secure website.

Industry and government can provide many forms of information that are beneficial to NCSD. First, identification of cyber points of contact within organizations allows the US–CERT to disseminate information on cyber threats and vulnerabilities to the appropriate parties. Second, industry reporting of any cyber incidents (e.g., worms, viruses, attacks, etc.) to the US–CERT provides NCSD the ability to enhance cyber situational awareness across all sectors as well as to provide alerts and warnings back to the public. In addition, of particular importance from the private sector is information about major impacts that affect critical infrastructure operations.

Third, the sharing of vulnerability assessment information with NCSD, including methodologies used, consequences of loss, and interdependencies, can assist NCSD in the identification of multi-sector cyber vulnerabilities and in collecting best practices that can be shared across sectors. Information on the cyber vulnerabilities the private sector is most concerned about, tactics that might be used to exploit these vulnerabilities, or the likelihood from their perspective that these vulnerabilities could be exploited, will assist NCSD in determining the state of cyber security for the IT Sector and the Nation. Fourth, it is important for NCSD to receive information on current protective measures, business continuity plans, and current levels of resources applied to cyber security. Insight into this information can enable NCSD to work even more effectively with industry to address vulnerabilities and further enhance protective measures. Fifth, NCSD is working with critical infrastructure owners and operators, vendors, and other security partners to promote control systems security. Information on control system architectures, protective measures, metrics, and research and development will further enhance NCSD's situational awareness and understanding of the state of control systems security and the ability to provide protective measures that are relevant and meaningful to the industry.

*Q2b. Are you currently receiving the information you need? What are the principal barriers to information sharing? Are changes in legislation or regulations needed to overcome these barriers?*

*A2b.* While NCSD does receive information from various stakeholders, we believe that we can improve upon our current level of analysis with more information. We continue to encourage companies, government agencies, and others to share information as described above.

Perhaps the greatest barrier to private sector information sharing with the government is concern about the possible release of shared information to the public, either unintentionally or by legal statute, such as the Freedom of Information Act (FOIA). There is a concern that the release of shared information by either means could potentially lead to the exploitation of any disclosed vulnerabilities by malicious actors, cause damage to corporate reputation, and/or result in legal consequences.

DHS, through the PCII program office, is pursuing ways to make the resulting program as effective as possible in furthering information sharing between the public and private sectors by providing industry protections and assurances through statutory exemption categories, as afforded by Congress.

*Q3. Response to Cyber Attacks*

*Q3a. If the information systems of a critical infrastructure company were attacked today, is the U.S. prepared to detect the attack and repel it or repair the systems quickly?*

*A3a.* Approximately eighty-five percent of the information infrastructure is owned and operated by the private sector; consequently, the majority of response activities reside with the private sector. In the case of attack on private sector infrastructure, NCSD's role includes providing support to the private sector in the form of warnings, incident response coordination, technical support, and coordination with law-enforcement as warranted. In addition, NCSD's US–CERT provides a national coordination center that links public and private response capabilities to facilitate information sharing across all infrastructure sectors and to help protect and maintain the continuity of our nation's cyber infrastructure. US–CERT serves as a 24x7x365 cyber watch, warning, and incident response center, and provides coordinated response to cyber incidents, a web portal for secure communications with private and public sector stakeholders, a daily report, a public website *(http://www.us-cert.gov/)*, and a National Cyber Alert System, which provides timely, actionable information to the public on both technical and non-technical bases. US–CERT also conducts malicious code analysis, provides malware technical support, and conducts cyber threat and vulnerability analysis. US–CERT works to advance relationships with infrastructure owners and operators to confirm attacks and enhance coordinated response activities.

In addition, if the attack rises to the level of a cyber incident of national significance, the National Cyber Response Coordination Group (NCRCG) will help to coordinate the federal response, including law enforcement and the intelligence community, with that of the private sector. NCSD co-chairs the NCRCG with the Department of Justice and the Department of Defense. An additional thirteen federal agencies with a statutory responsibility for and/or specific capability toward cyber security, including the intelligence community, are members. NCSD serves as the Executive Agent and point of contact for the NCRCG. As directed by Homeland Security Presidential Directives 5 and 8, NCSD helped to create a *Cyber Annex* to the *National Response Plan* (NRP)[1] that provides a framework for responding to cyber incidents of national significance. The *Cyber Annex* establishes the NCRCG as the principal Federal Government cyber response body.

The government is prepared to respond to major cyber incidents in coordination with the private sector and is working to formalize incident response coordination by ensuring that standard operating procedures work in unison. NCSD is also working to facilitate, enhance, and ensure public-private coordination during major cyber incidents.

*Q3b. What about if it were an attack on the Internet?*

*A3b.* As stated above, because approximately 85 percent of the information infrastructure is owned and operated by private industry, the majority of mitigation and restoration activity is borne by private industry. In this regard, NCSD's US–CERT is enhancing relationships with Internet owners, operators, and other associated industries to aide in incident coordination and communications with all players to facilitate rapid response to a significant cyber event or incident. Specifically, the US–CERT maintains regular communications with the Information Technology Information Sharing and Analysis Center (ISAC) and the Telecommunications ISAC. Additionally, US–CERT has established relationships with the Financial and Multi-State ISACs and is well coordinated with the ISAC Council that includes ISACs from other critical infrastructures. US–CERT is prepared to reach out and alert those within the ISAC communities and affected infrastructure sectors when necessary.

A large-scale attack on the infrastructure of the Internet may constitute a cyber incident of national significance that would activate the NCRCG. The NCRCG is also building a more robust partnership with the IT sector, with Internet Service Providers, and through NCSD's responsibilities for the cyber component of the National Infrastructure Protection Plan (NIPP) to enable a collaborative, coordinated approach to attack mitigation and recovery.

The NCSD also co-chairs the Internet Disruption Working Group (IDWG) with the National Communications Systems (NCS). The IDWG was established by the NCSD and NCS to form a strategic partnership with other key government agencies. Its focus is to identify and detail actions that can be taken in the near-term to enhance Internet resilience. An initial goal of the IDWG was to reach out to private sector stakeholders. A one-day IDWG Forum was conducted on November 29, 2005 as an initial undertaking to bring subject matter experts together around a common concern: Internet disruption and hardening with a focus on gathering feedback on the most likely risk scenarios facing the Internet infrastructure today. Emphasis was placed on discussing immediate near-term needs and requirements for industry-government coordination in preparation for or during an Internet disruption of national significance. The IDWG will analyze outcome data from the forum to develop near-term action plans for risk preparedness, vulnerability mitigation, and response and reconstitution. Information will be provided to the NCS, NCRCG and the US–CERT for consideration as input to the update of the NRP/ESF–2 which is the overarching National plan for communications recovery/reconstitution activities. Near-term action plans are scheduled to be completed by the end of the 2nd quarter, FY06.

*Q3c. What role can and should DHS and other public and private organizations play in these response activities?*

*A3c.* Although the private sector owns and operates such a large part of the information infrastructure, and that infrastructure represents a critical national asset, response activities reside with both the private sector and the government. DHS's role is to ensure the coordination and effectiveness of government preparedness and response efforts in partnership with the private sector.

US–CERT is the operational arm for DHS's coordinated cyber preparedness and response and collaborates with affected parties to assist with rapid response. US–CERT also builds situational awareness, provides malicious code and vulnerability analysis, disseminates timely alerts and warnings, participates in exercises, develops and refines standard operating procedures, and provides training.

---

[1] *http://www.dhs.gov/dhspublicldisplay?theme=15&content=4269*

As discussed above, the *Cyber Annex* to the *National Response Plan* (NRP), which provides a framework for responding to cyber incidents of national significance, establishes the NCRCG as the principal Federal Government response body. The NCRCG will engage the applicable private sector entities to ensure both the feasibility and comprehensiveness of the mitigation and recovery strategy.

*Q3d. What are the barriers to DHS, companies, or other organizations providing a quick, effective, and coordinated response?*

*A3d.* NCSD views the current challenges to include clearly defined roles and responsibilities for response activities. Delineating roles and responsibilities between the public and private sectors with regard to response is well underway. The US–CERT Concept of Operations (CONOPS) provides federal agency reporting and coordination, while the NCRCG CONOPS provides response to a cyber incident of national significance. US–CERT and NCRCG continue to refine draft Standard Operating Procedures (SOPS) to ensure systemization and coordination of response actions. Also, as stated above, NCSD is working to facilitate, enhance, and ensure public-private coordination during major cyber incidents.

NCSD's Cyber Storm exercise seeks to test whether in the event of an incident, the public and private sectors are prepared to act in a coordinated fashion. By examining homeland security cyber response and recovery mechanisms, NCSD can evaluate the existing resources and procedures to recommend improvements to information sharing, processes, and policies for a more coordinated and robust national cyber incident preparedness and response. Specifically, Cyber Storm will provide the opportunity for the lead agencies in the Federal Government to examine their SOPS and CONOPS in a controlled environment and make revisions based on the outcome of the exercise.

*Q4. Cyber Security R&D*

*Q4a. What are the biggest technology gaps, or areas where research and development (R&D) are most needed, that you see in trying to protect information systems across critical infrastructure sectors?*

*A4a.* For cyber security research and development (R&D) within the Department of Homeland Security, the Science and Technology (S&T) Directorate coordinates with the National Cyber Security Division (NCSD). NCSD collects, develops, and submits cyber security R&D requirements to provide input for the S&T Directorate's cyber security research priorities and to the federal cyber security R&D community. The most significant technology gaps where R&D is needed to protect information systems across critical infrastructure sectors fall into three categories: (1) technologies that are applicable to standard network-based information systems, [the Department of Homeland Security's (DHS) Science and Technology (S&T) Directorate is addressing some of these through existing and planned programs within the Cyber Security portfolio]; (2) technologies that are applicable to distributed control systems [the S&T Directorate is addressing these issues through existing programs within the Critical Infrastructure portfolio—see Q02935]; and (3) technologies that are relevant when enterprise information systems are directly connected to distributed control systems.

Technologies needing further R&D related to distributed control systems are:

— Efficient, intelligent, cross-domain intrusion detection systems
— Effective authentication and authorization technologies
— Methods for testing and verification of solutions to retrofit existing systems
— Automated security assessments
— Efficient, low-cost encryption technologies
— Improved technologies for non-intrusive testing methods for secondary (supervisory) instrumentation systems.

Improved technologies needing further R&D related to enterprise systems connected to distributed control systems, but are not currently commercially available are:

— System-wide intrusion detection and prevention systems
— Intelligent firewalls
— Multi-level security systems
— High-level auditing and reporting systems

The *Federal Plan for Cyber Security and Information Assurance Research and Development* (CSIA R&D Plan) marks the Federal Government's first step toward developing an agenda for the R&D listed above. The Plan responds to significant drivers for improved federal cyber security and information assurance R&D arising from current federal priorities, as outlined in the 2005 report of the President's Information Technology Advisory Committee (PITAC) and, additionally, the following documents: the OSTP/OMB Memorandum on Interagency R&D Priorities for FY 2007; *Cyber Security: A Crisis of Prioritization,* the 2003 *National Strategy to Secure Cyberspace;* and the 2002 *Cyber Security Research and Development Act* (Public Law 107–305). The purpose of the Plan is to provide baseline information and an initial technical framework for a coordinated multi-agency R&D effort in cyber security and information assurance. The Plan was developed by the Cyber Security and Information Assurance Interagency Working Group (CSIA IWG) of the National Science and Technology Council (NSTC). The CSIA R&D Plan has been coordinated, and is consistent with the National Critical Infrastructure Protection Research and Development Plan, developed by OSTP and the S&T Directorate.

The CSIA IWG was established by the Subcommittee on Infrastructure and the Subcommittee on Networking and Information Technology Research and Development (NITRD). The purpose of the IWG is to coordinate policy, programs, and budgets for cyber security and information assurance (CSIA) R&D. This includes identifying and integrating requirements, conducting joint program planning, and developing joint strategies for the CSIA R&D programs conducted by agency members of the Subcommittees. For the purposes of this document, CSIA includes fundamental and applied R&D, technology development and engineering, demonstrations, testing and evaluation, and education and training; and "agencies" refers to federal departments, agencies, directorates, institutes, and other organizational entities.

The following federal agencies are represented on the IWG:

- Department of Commerce:
  - National Institute of Standards and Technology
- Department of Defense:
  - Office of the Deputy Under Secretary of Defense for Science & Technology
  - Defense Information Systems Agency
  - Defense Advanced Research Projects Agency
  - Departments of the Air Force, Army, and Navy
  - National Security Agency
  - Technical Support Working Group (joint with Department of State)
- Department of Energy
- Department of Health and Human Services:
  - National Institutes of Health
- Department of Homeland Security:
  - National Communications System
  - National Cyber Security Division
  - Science and Technology Directorate
- Department of Justice
- Department of State
- Department of Transportation:
  - Federal Aviation Administration
- Department of the Treasury
- Central Intelligence Agency
- Environmental Protection Agency
- National Aeronautics and Space Administration
- National Science Foundation

*Q4b. What federal R&D programs exist in these areas and what are their funding levels?*

*A4b.* We refer you to the *Federal Plan for Cyber Security and Information Assurance Research and Development* (CSIA R&D Plan) for a consolidated list of R&D programs in the areas listed above, broken out by federal agency. The Plan also includes detailed funding information for each of the programs.

The federal agency funding information gathered during the CSIA Plan process was pre-decisional and of varying granularity; it was collected only to provide a preliminary indication of federal agency spending emphases in cyber security and information assurance. Thus, the baseline findings derived from this information should be viewed as useful in the aggregate, but not a comprehensive source of detailed investment data.

DHS's S&T Directorate and the Office of Science and Technology Policy (OSTP) prepare an annual Critical Infrastructure Protection (CIP) R&D Plan, as mandated by Homeland Security Presidential Directive (HSPD)–7. The first of these plans is available to the public. It specifically addresses and combines ongoing R&D activities and future goals for both cyber and physical domains. This plan has been thoroughly coordinated across multiple federal agencies and includes input from the private sector, academia, and the national laboratories through a series of facilitated technical workshops. The plan was developed under the auspices of the Infrastructure Subcommittee of the National Science and Technology Council (NSTC), overseen by OSTP. The subcommittee further acts as an integrating mechanism for input and planning efforts conducted by two interagency working groups, one focused on physical security and one focused on cyber security, that report to the Subcommittee.

Within the DHS S&T Directorate, the CIP and Cyber Security portfolios have several programs linking cyber security research to critical infrastructure protection:

- *Process Control System Forum (PCSF)*—This forum was established this year to accelerate the development of technology that will enhance the security, safety, and reliability of process control system (PCS) and supervisory control and data acquisition (SCADA) systems. The Forum provides a united venue for industry and government (including DHS's S&T Directorate, DHS's National Cyber Security Division, and other partners) to work together in evaluating, specifying, developing, refining, and testing new technologies. The S&T Directorate has expended $1.5M in FY 2004, and obligated another $1.5M in FY 2005. In FY 2006, it is anticipated that an additional $750K will be used to fund PCSF.
- *Control System Security Test Center (CSSTC)*—In collaboration with the Department of Energy (DOE) and its resources and testing facilities, this program focuses on developing procedures for enumerating the vulnerability of process control systems to cyber attack and finding solutions to correct these weaknesses. This is intended to be a close private/public partnership effort with the critical infrastructure industries that use and manufacture process control systems. The CSSTC is run out of the National Cyber Security Division; funding does not come from the Science and Technology Directorate.
- *Linking the Oil & Gas Industry to Improve Cyber-Security (LOGIC)*—This public-private partnership is aimed at reducing vulnerabilities in process control environments used in the oil and gas sector by establishing a framework for assessing risks, evaluating new technologies, and providing an environment for collaborative cyber-security projects. Currently in planning stages, this effort brings together government and private sector stakeholders to identify a working model for leveraging the collective resources of the oil and gas sector, government agencies, and national laboratories to improve process control system security. In FY 2006, the S&T Directorate intends to fund LOGIC and $500K.
- *Small Business Innovative Research (SBIR) Awards*—In FY 2004, 13 Phase I SBIR projects were awarded in the area of process control system security. In FY 2005, Phase II SBIRs were awarded to a subset of the Phase I performers, on the following topics:
  - — Advanced Security for SCADA Systems;
  - — Protection of SCADA Systems Using Physics Based Authentication and Location Awareness;
  - — Improved Security Information Management for SCADA Systems;
  - — A Robust Secure Management System for SCADA/EMS Operations; and
  - — A Toolkit for Next Generation Electric Power SCADA Security Protection and Research.

In SBIRs for SCADA/Process Control Security, the S&T Directorate has committed/obligated approximately $3.75M for the Phase II efforts.

**Questions submitted by Representative Bart Gordon**

*Q1. Earlier this year, GAO reported to Congress (GAO–05–827T) that the Department of Homeland Security "has not yet developed national cyber threat and vulnerability assessments or government/industry contingency recovery plans for cyber security, including a plan for recovering key Internet functions."*

*Q1a. What is the current status of progress toward developing national cyber threat and vulnerability assessments, and by what date or dates do you estimate such assessments will be completed?*

*A1a.* As part of NCSD's participation in the development of the National Infrastructure Protection Plan (NIPP), the NIPP Base Plan discusses cyber security and the cross-sector cyber element of critical infrastructure and key resources protection across all 17 critical infrastructure sectors. It also highlights cyber security concerns in an appendix that provides additional details on processes, procedures, and mechanisms needed to achieve NIPP goals and the supporting objectives for cyber security. The cyber security appendix specifies cyber responsibilities for security partners, processes and initiatives to reduce cyber risk, and milestones and metrics to measure progress on enhancing the Nation's protection of cyber infrastructure.

The draft NIPP Base Plan was released for final review and comment on November 2, 2005 and addresses the federal, State, territorial, tribal, local, and private sector roles and responsibilities for critical infrastructure protection. It will be completed in early 2006. The 17 critical infrastructure and key resource (CI/KR) Sector-Specific Plans (SSPs) will further detail risk reduction strategies related to their respective critical cyber infrastructure. The SSPs will be completed in 180 days after the publication of the NIPP Base Plan.

In addition to physical risk and vulnerability assessments, there are a number of DHS initiatives underway that examine cyber-related vulnerabilities. DHS, in coordination with the private sector, is identifying cyber vulnerability assessment best practices. This effort began with an evaluation of various methodologies from across public and private sectors. NCSD is also working closely with other DHS components to ensure that cyber aspects of threat, consequence, and vulnerability analysis are consistently and appropriately included in risk methodology efforts. These efforts include the Risk Analysis and Management for Critical Asset Protection (RAMCAP), the Vulnerability Identification Self Assessment Tool, Comprehensive Reviews, and Site Assistance Visits. To achieve this objective, NCSD will:

1) Support the development of cyber components of RAMCAP.
2) Complete its evaluation of public and private sector vulnerability assessment methodologies and document best practices in Q1FY06 for integration into other efforts;
3) Integrate cyber issues and best practices into DHS risk management and vulnerability assessment methods and tools through ongoing and continued collaboration and coordination with DHS entities as methods and tools are implemented; and
4) enhance understanding of the impact of cyber attacks by analyzing the consequences (i.e., economic, human, physical) of cyber attacks on critical infrastructure sectors by Q3FY06.

In addition, NCSD's US–CERT Control Systems Security Program and the US–CERT Control Systems Security Center (CSSC) work to reduce control system vulnerabilities in our critical infrastructure. The Control Systems Security Program coordinates efforts among Federal, State, and local governments, as well as control system owners, operators, and vendors to improve control system security within and across all critical infrastructure sectors by reducing cyber security vulnerabilities and risk. The US–CERT CSSC coordinates control system incident management, provides timely situational awareness information, and manages control system vulnerability and threat reduction activities. The US–CERT CSSC brings together government, industry, and academia to reduce vulnerabilities, respond to threats, and foster public/private collaboration. NCSD and the Control Systems Security Program are also working with other DHS components to ensure that control systems security is integrated into risk and vulnerability assessment methodologies and tools designed for use across multiple sectors.

Further, to reduce control system vulnerabilities in our critical infrastructure, CSSC developed a draft cyber security protection framework for identifying control systems security protection measures and comparing them against existing security standards. The framework provides a systematic methodology for assessing the cyber security posture of control systems. It is designed to reduce the burden on owners and operators by providing them with a means to select protective measures that apply to their specific architecture and operating environment and reduce their respective risk.

As part of this framework, the CSSC also has capabilities at Idaho National Laboratory to perform vulnerability assessments of control systems. The CSSC is working with commercial vendors and Department of Energy (DOE) to complete assessments of three different control systems to identify cyber vulnerabilities, reverse engineer exploits, and provide solutions to secure vendor systems. A code-based analysis has also been conducted in cooperation with a vendor/manufacturer to identify possible vulnerabilities and recommendations to secure the system.

The cyber security protection framework also leverages best practices from industry for securing control systems against cyber attacks and organizes them so the control systems community can identify specific solutions to their security vulnerabilities. As part of the framework, implementation tools, such as a "self-assessment tool," have also been developed to allow owners and operators of industrial control systems to perform on-site self-assessments against a database of categorized security requirements.

In addition, NCSD's Law Enforcement/Intelligence Branch has multiple efforts underway in this area. For example, the Law Enforcement/Intelligence Branch, in collaboration with the Homeland Infrastructure Threat and Risk Assessment Center, (HITRAC), has created a draft Domestic Cyber Risk Estimate to evaluate the threats emanating from inside the U.S., to complement international threat assessments completed by the intelligence community. HITRAC is comprised of subject matter experts from the Office of Infrastructure Protection and the Office of Intelligence and Analysis.

*Q1b. What is the current status of progress toward developing government/industry contingency recovery plans for cyber security, including a plan for recovering key Internet functions, and by what date or dates do you estimate such recovery plans will be completed?*

*A1b.* DHS is confronting this security challenge through the work of the Internet Disruption Working Group (IDWG), a partnership between the NCSD and the National Communications System (NCS). To initiate the substantive work of IDWG, the NCSD conducted a one-day IDWG Forum with major public sector partners and subject matter experts in late November 2005. Participants at the Forum will work to continue to collaboratively work in identifying actions that can be taken in the near-term to better protect against, respond to, and reconstitute following an Internet disruption. Topics discussed included: risk scenarios; path forward/near-term protective measures; key Internet infrastructure components; path forward/near-term response; scope of disruption analysis (or "thresholds"); and path forward/near-term response.

The IDWG will analyze outcome data to develop near-term action plans for risk preparedness, situational awareness, vulnerability mitigation, and response and reconstitution. Information will be provided to the NCS, NCRCG, and the US–CERT for consideration as input to the update of the National Response Plan (NRP)/Emergency Support Function (ESF) #2, which is the overarching National plan for communications recovery/reconstitution activities. Near-term action plans are scheduled to be completed by the end of the 2nd quarter, FY06. Action plans will be composed detailing near-term steps for industry and government to increase Internet resiliency.

In addition, the Emergency Support Function #2, Communications, is one of fifteen emergency support functions (ESF) maintained by the Federal Emergency Management Agency (FEMA) as part of the Federal Response Plan (FRP). The National Communications System (NCS) is responsible for ESF #2, which ensures the federal telecommunications support to federal, State and local response efforts following a Presidentially declared major disaster, emergency or extraordinary situation under the FRP. Because the Internet backbone is telecom-based, NCS's expertise will help to promote the survivability of the Internet and recovery after disruption. NCSD and NCS have agreed to explore the need for possible recommendations to revise ESF–2 to ensure that cyber is appropriately accounted for (with SOPs as appropriate).

*Q2. The Critical Infrastructure Information (CII) program, which is authorized by the statute creating the Department of Homeland Security (DHS), is intended to protect cyber security related information provided voluntarily to DHS by the private sector. In response to a question at the hearing, you indicated that DHS has interim rules in place for instituting the CII program.*

*Q2a. What is the current status of the CII program and by what date do you estimate that the final rule for its implementation will be in place?*

*A2a.* The Department has synthesized the comments received and has reviewed the operating experience with the program to date. The item has a very high priority; however, DHS is committed to making sure that the rule and the Program work effectively for the Department and critical infrastructure owners/operators, and thus, the draft document has been undergoing further refinement. In the meantime, based on its operating experience, the PCII Program Office has already been implementing changes in its operating procedures to respond to some of the issues raised in the comments to make PCII more flexible/useful for submitters. The editing process is nearing completion. Before going to the Federal Register, the Rule must be submitted to OMB for interagency coordination. The Department is committed to working to resolve any issues that may arise there as quickly as possible. The rule will be published as a Final Rule and DHS will continue to work with submitters and government users to address implementation issues as they arise.

In addition to these efforts toward a Final Rule, approximately a year ago, DHS' PCII Office implemented a way for companies to sign up to submit protected critical infrastructure information to NCSD on a recurring basis through the secure US–CERT Portal. Since then, NCSD has been working toward a mechanism to enable companies to submit protected information on an episodic basis, rather than having to pre-enroll. This mechanism is scheduled to be implemented in early 2006. Additionally, the Department has been working to establish a pilot with the NCSD/US–CERT submissions to allow the submitter to request limited dissemination of their information. This effort is expected to be active in early 2006 as well.

*Q2b. What are the principal concerns of the private sector thus far regarding implementation of the CII program, and how is DHS responding to these concerns?*

*A2b.* One of the main concerns frequently expressed by the private sector with respect to the PCII Program is dissemination of information shared by the private sector. Several organizations have stated that they would contemplate sharing cyber related information with NCSD if dissemination of their information were limited to only NCSD. As a result, NCSD has begun working with the PCII Program Office in 'piloting' the capability for an entity to submit CII information directly to NCSD and request that information be limited in its dissemination to only NCSD. We expect this pilot effort, consistent with the interim final rule, to be operational shortly.

*Q3. In his testimony, Mr. Freese indicated that the Process Control Security Forum is doing good work in developing design guidelines for the next generation of more secure control systems, and he suggested the need for support from DHS for seed money to support the implementation of ideas and concepts developed by the Forum.*

*What is your view of the value of the Process Control Security Forum, and what is your response to Mr. Freese's suggestion?*

*A3.* The Process Control Systems Forum (PCSF) is an industry lead group comprised of many interest and working groups with the focus of securing legacy and next generation control systems. The PCSF is sponsored by the Department of Homeland Security's Science & Technology (S&T) Directorate. The NCSD co-chairs the PCSF and supports the PCSF in their mission to accelerate the design, development, and deployment of more secure control and legacy systems currently embedded with our nation's critical infrastructure. The NCSD Control Systems Security Program's (CSSP) goal is to reduce the risk from a cyber attack to control systems associated with our nation's critical infrastructure. The NCSD CSSP provides recommendations for areas of research and development (R&D) to the S&T Directorate as gaps and vulnerabilities are identified in control system cyber security.

NCSD's CSSP is an active participant within the PCSF. The CSSP leads several interest groups within the PCSF in order to inform and receive comments on CSSP initiatives, such as the Control Systems Security Framework and Self-Assessment tool and control systems security focused standards. The value of the PSCF is its ability to reach out to representatives of the critical infrastructure sectors, such as chemical, water, energy, and telecommunications, which utilize Process Control Systems (PCS) and Supervisory Control and Data Acquisition (SCADA). The NCSD actively engages with the PSCF to reach vendors and asset owners as part of its outreach efforts. More recently, for example, the NCSD CSSP published the *Hurricane Katrina Control Systems Assistance Informational Paper,* which provided guidance for rebuilding and securely restarting control systems. The paper is available on the PCSF website, as well as the NCSD US–CERT website.

**Question submitted by Representative Eddie Bernice Johnson**

*Q1. I understand that the Secretary of Homeland Security created the new position of Assistant Secretary of Cyber Security and Telecommunications. Why has this position not yet been filled, and when will it be filled?*

*A1.* As with other key leadership positions, the Assistant Secretary for Cyber Security and Telecommunications position requires a unique skill set of managerial and substantive expertise and we are in the process of reviewing the qualifications of several candidates. The Department will move forward with the process of identifying a suitable nominee as quickly as possible.

ANSWERS TO POST-HEARING QUESTIONS

*Responses by John S. Leggate, Chief Information Officer and Group Vice President, Digital & Communications Technology, BP Plc., United Kingdom*

**Questions submitted by Chairman Sherwood L. Boehlert**

*Q1. Measuring Cyber Security*

*Q1a. How do you measure your company's cyber security?*

*A1a.* We assess our capability to manage security vs. the risk, assessed through a combination of assessment of threats against the company, the potential weaknesses in systems and processes and the impact that such exposures could have.

*Q1b. How do determine if your company's level of cyber vulnerability is being reduced?*

*A1b.* The assessment approach stated above measures risk reduction activities such as device patching and the relevance of such actions.

*Q1c. How do you decide what is "secure enough"?*

*A1c.* The impact assessment, measuring financial and non-financial impact (such as safety, environment, effect on society, regulatory compliance and reputation) determines whether something matters to the company. The likelihood of the event, assessed by threat intelligence and effectiveness of controls determines how much action needs to be taken.

*Q1d. Are there specific metrics you use in evaluating the cyber security of your company?*

*A1d.* We use specific metrics relating to the effectiveness of particular controls or the trend of threats. We have a scale used for assessing impact for the most significant risks. (Broader concepts such as value at risk have as yet proved illusory in the case of operational risks).

*Q1e. How should the Department of Homeland Security (DHS) determine if the Nation is making progress?*

*A1e.* Firstly, through risk assessment of security—what is at risk and how well is it protected, the capabilities deployed, measured in the form of skilled people, deployed security technologies and processes. Secondly through the number of security events being reported.

*Q1f. Are government mandates needed to increase the progress and get to "secure enough"?*

*A1f.* The government should always avoid mandating specifics, as true knowledge of the most appropriate control always exists within the sector (no matter which sector). However, government should mandate processes and actions that ensure that cross-sector risks are identified and picked up and that sectors measure themselves against their own standards.

*Business Case for Cyber Security*

*Q1g. Within your company, how do you make the business case for the costs associated with more secure information technology products? What can the Federal Government do to help you make this case and make investment in cyber security more attractive?*

*A1g.* The security requirements for information technology products are generally little more than the basics of good integrity, i.e., no vulnerabilities. The addition of simple security measures like frrewalls and anti-virus and next generation protection of data is just good business. No special action is required outside normal good business practice. The government need take no additional action.

*Q2. Information Sharing*

*Q2a. What information would you find most helpful to receive from the government (especially DHS) or from other companies when you are making decisions related to what cyber security you need. When responding to an attack or an incident?*

*A2a.* Threat information about new risks and problems being encountered in near real-time.

*Q2b. What information have you been asked for by DHS that you feel uncomfortable providing and why?*

*A2b.* Detail of security events and known vulnerabilities. We have no assurances as to the protection of our information, who has access to it and how it will be used. Additionally we are concerned that there will be demands put on the individuals dealing with the incident that are no in the best interest of our company.

*Q2c. What are the principal barriers to information sharing: Are changes in the legislation or regulations needed to overcome these barriers?*

*A2c.* Simple trust between one person and another. It takes time to build and needs processes to bed in before it works. Changes in process such as a move from ISACs to central DHS actions was a backward step in this fragile trust model. Government funding to help the information sharing infrastructure is invaluable in getting over the lead time between starting and seeing value (which is a barrier for company funding).

*Q3. Responding to Cyber attacks*

*Q3a. If the information systems of a critical infrastructure company were attacked today, is the U.S. prepared to detect the attack and repel it or repair the systems quickly?*

*A3a.* It depends on the industry, the nature of the attack and the company itself. Response would range from excellent to poor. As a whole the U.S. Government would probably not be of much help in helping critical infrastructure companies; however, the company themselves may be prepared to handle the majority of attacks.

*Q3b. What about if it were an attack on the Internet?*

*A3b.* There is no coordinated response to an Internet attack. Recovery would be by adhoc action and if unlucky could be catastrophic if the impact spread across sectors. Lots of very good technical people work on an adhoc basis but there is NO strategic plan or coordinated effort.

*Q3c. What role can and should DHS and other public and private organizations play in these response activities?*

*A3c.* DHS itself can do little in the response, this has to be done by the companies that own the infrastructure itself. DHS can help best in analysis, preparedness and planning.

*Q3d. What are the barriers to DHS, companies or other organizations providing a quick, effective and coordinated response?*

*A3d.* Poor planning and lack of understanding of interdependencies and weak points but most of all TRUST. DHS has done little to foster trust with the critical infrastructure companies.

*Q4. International Cyber Security*

*Q4a. In your experience working with multiple Federal Governments on cyber security, what notable differences exist between the approach of the U.S. and that of other countries?*

*A4a.* The U.S. approach is paradoxical, there seems to be good funding in total but this is not integrated into a focused program. The lack of continuity and lack of seniority in the cyber security part of DHS has led to fragmentation of the program with many activities being started but few big wins to point at. Cyber Security has taken a back seat especially in R&D—DHS S&T is only spending about $15 million on cyber security.

*Q4b. Are other countries supporting activities that the U.S. should be doing too?*

*A4b.* Delivery of specifics such as practical solutions from funded research, novel cyber-intelligence, and user-led security solutions fora have all been seen to add great value in the programs of some other countries.

*Q5. What is the Department of Homeland Security doing to foster private sector efforts in cyber security and what could the agency do that it is not doing now?*

*A5.* The ISACs presented a great opportunity for private sector engagement, but DHS has programmatically eliminated independent ISACs. The initiatives should be given focus and direction to have specific rather than generic work programs.

*Q6. Are effective practices procedures and technologies now available to guard against the adverse impacts of cyberspace vulnerabilities?*

*A6.* As we digitize more and more we need to have a significant improvement in software engineering to create systems of adequate integrity. This philosophy is still not present in the IT industry.

*Q7. Are there shortcomings for particular critical infrastructure areas?*

*A7.* As traditional process control technologies such as SCADA/DCS continue to integrate with Commercial Off The Shelf IT systems we see vulnerabilities and threats being introduced into environments that cannot be changed to deal with them. A new class of co-existing security protection is required to address legacy systems until such time as new, built-secure technologies can take their place.

ANSWERS TO POST-HEARING QUESTIONS

*Responses by David E. Kepler, Corporate Vice President of Shared Services and Chief Information Officer, The Dow Chemical Company*

**Questions submitted by Chairman Sherwood L. Boehlert**

*Q1. Measuring Cyber security*

- *How do you measure your company's cyber security?*
- *How do determine if your company's level of cyber vulnerability is being reduced?*
- *How do you decide what is "secure enough"?*
- *Are there specific metrics you use in evaluating the cyber security of your company?*
- *How should the Department of Homeland Security (DHS) determine if the Nation is making progress?*
- *Are government mandates needed to increase the progress and get to "secure enough"?*

*A1.* Dow Chemical has a disciplined process to manage risk and address cyber security in our company. The metrics established in this framework allow us to analyze our effectiveness against priorities, understand internal support for addressing these priorities, and identify strengths and areas for improvement in our efforts. This framework also provides a valuable mechanism to compare our own priorities and self-assessments against those of peer companies. Our processes are based on industry standards and best practices.

Today's world requires us to maintain constant vigilance and effort to ensure our security. There is no foreseeable point where we as a company can declare we are "secure enough." We must continue to assess our risk and vulnerabilities applying the necessary investments, resources and management systems to effectively manage risk and mitigate vulnerabilities on an on-going basis.

The Department of Homeland Security (DHS) cannot be everything to everyone. Instead, it is in our national interest for DHS to place a priority and focus on cyber threats of significant consequence that could interrupt our nation's critical information and communications infrastructure or cause significant disruption to our economy. DHS should be measured by how well they plan, defend, and respond to such threats of national consequence.

*Q2. Business Case for Cyber Security*

*Within your company, how do you make the business case for the costs associated with more secure information technology products? What can the Federal Government do to help you make this case and make investment in cyber security more attractive?*

*A2.* Information systems are critical to Dow Chemical's business operations and are integral to the competitive advantage of our company. Ensuring the reliability and security of our systems, processes, and information is of the utmost importance. The business case for cyber security is very simple for us. If our critical information systems or manufacturing control systems are compromised, our ability to conduct business is compromised. Investments are based on impact to our current operations and stakeholders, not for benefit return.

*Q3. Information Sharing*

- *What information would you find most helpful to receive from the government (especially DHS) or from other companies when you are making decisions related to what cyber security you need. When responding to an attack or an incident?*
- *What information have you been asked for by DHS that you feel uncomfortable providing and why?*
- *What are the principal barriers to information sharing: Are changes in the legislation or regulations needed to overcome these barriers?*

*A3.* DHS should strive to provide specific information regarding pending threats, likely attacks, and recommended response plans where possible. Although understanding this is not always feasible, it is necessary to have an ongoing, two-way dialogue with critical infrastructure sectors on the current threat environment, likely trends, and potential mitigation options.

We believe DHS has established programs, such as PCII, and continues to revise theses programs as necessary to enable the effective sharing of information from the private sector to DHS. However, we believe DHS and the private sector communications need to be protected in both directions to enable dialogue on highly sensitive areas. PCII only protects information we submit, it does not promote reverse sharing. An additional concern is the growing number of requests from federal agencies outside DHS and State agencies for security and proprietary sensitive information that could otherwise be protected as PCII. If requested under broad authority granted by various laws and statutes, the information would be considered "independently obtained," and would not be protected under existing DHS programs.

Further, even programs within DHS, such as protection of SSI, are not consistent with PCII and do not offer equivalent protections. Efforts must be taken to harmonize the protection of information within DHS and across all governmental agencies to ensure that critical security information is not compromised and that development of important security information and sharing of such information is encouraged. We believe that DHS should be empowered as the central agency responsible for the protection of security sensitive and proprietary sensitive information. Redundant requests from other agencies should be limited, and if information sharing is required across federal, state and local agencies, it must have the same level of protections provided by PCII.

*Q4. Responding to Cyber attacks*

- *If the information systems of a critical infrastructure company were attacked today, is the U.S. prepared to detect the attack and repel it or repair the systems quickly?*
- *What about if it were an attack on the Internet?*
- *What role can and should DHS and other public and private organizations play in these response activities?*
- *What are the barriers to DHS, companies or other organizations providing a quick, effective and coordinated response?*

*A4.* The U.S. must be prepared to address high consequence cyber attacks to our nation's critical information and communications infrastructure. Research and development efforts need to be focused on how best to anticipate and model, detect, defend, and respond to significant interruptions to the Internet and communications infrastructure. More needs to be done to focus attention on these high risk concerns—ensuring adequate planning, resources, and management structure are in place to respond to these high-risk scenarios. Less engagement in security and reliability solutions is needed as this is being addressed by marketplace forces.

**Questions submitted by Representative Eddie Bernice Johnson**

*Q1. What is the Department of Homeland Security doing to foster greater private sector efforts in cyber security and what could the agency do that it is not doing now?*

*A1.* DHS is currently initiating a number of projects they believe will increase cyber security in the private sector. However, these efforts are not well coordinated with the private sector and appear to lack coordination within the agency itself. A chartered engagement with the Chemical Sector's Security Program is needed to understand and address the highest areas of risk to our country as it relates to the chemical sector.

*Q2. Are effective practices, procedures, and technologies now available to guard against the adverse impacts of cyberspace vulnerabilities? Are there shortcomings for particular critical infrastructure areas?*

*A2.* Speaking for the chemical industry, we have established the Chemical Sector Cyber Security Program to create guidance and reference procedures as well as best practices across our industry. For over three years, this program has actively engaged to educate large and small chemical companies and to build guidance into industry programs such as the Responsible Care Security Code.

Although technology is improving, the current approach of releasing software and infrastructure with security vulnerabilities that requires patching later must be addressed. Information technology providers must more thoroughly test their products for existing security threats and apply necessary protections against anticipated future threats. The market appears to be working—incenting companies to provide much more secure software and systems. However, if this trend does not continue, government intervention may be needed to ensure information technology is fully developed and secured before being released into the marketplace. Companies have the financial capability to address this, and government sponsored R&D should not be required.

ANSWERS TO POST-HEARING QUESTIONS

*Responses by Gerald S. Freese, Director of Enterprise Information Security, American Electric Power*

**Questions submitted by Chairman Sherwood L. Boehlert**

*Q1. Measuring Cyber Security*

*Q1a. How do you measure your company's cyber security?*

*A1a.* Measurement is most effective against a backdrop consisting of a security policy and standards. Measurement is accomplished in several ways, depending on the intended focus:

- Compliance with internal security standards—measured against metrics derived from self-imposed security requirements (based on business drivers and best practices).
- Compliance with regulatory requirements—measured against externally generated security mandates (Sarbanes Oxley, HIPAA, FERC, GLB, etc.).
- Penetration testing—Tests technical security architecture for vulnerabilities. Provides multiple levels of security gap determinations and direction for remediation.

*Q1b. How do you determine if your company's level of cyber vulnerability is being reduced?*

*A1b.* Using periodic scanning of networks, servers and workstation for known vulnerabilities; ongoing compliance checks determine levels of compliance with standards. Compliance checks rely on the use of technical and process metrics developed through best practices or regulatory requirements.

*Q1c. How do you decide what is secure enough?*

*A1c.* "Secure enough" is determined through analysis of several variables; these are risk to business systems, regulatory requirements and the level of security implemented in the technical architecture.

*Q1d. How should DHS determine if the Nation is making progress?*

*A1d.* DHS must continue to work toward comprehensive information sharing with critical infrastructure industries. The NIPP is an excellent start toward greater co-operation but the PCII program needs to be fully implemented and socialized to be effective.

*Q1e. Are government mandates needed to increase the progress and get to "secure enough?"*

*A1e.* Critical infrastructure industries do not want government mandates to increase security. Unfortunately, there is no way for the government to effectively help protect critical infrastructure if its components do not have some consistency in the level of risk-based protection they have in place. I feel that at some point in the future, government will step in and establish federal requirements. Hopefully they will do it with full industry collaboration.

*Q2. Business Case for Cyber Security*

*Q2a. Within your company, how do you make the business case for the costs associated with more secure information technology products?*

*A2a.* In several ways: Regulatory or legislative requirements; Risk identification and mitigation; Cultivating strong executive support for CI protection.

*Q2b. What can the Federal Government do to help make this case?*

*A2b.* The government can provide more pertinent, substantiated threat information. They can also design financial assistance for selected protective measures. These would have to be accomplished with extensive collaboration with the private sector.

*Q3. Information Sharing*

*Q3a. What information would you find most helpful to receive from the government (especially DHS) or from other companies when you are making decisions related to what cyber security you need? When responding to an attack or an incident?*

*A3a.* In question two, we discussed that there is a need for more pertinent and substantiated threat information from the government. When responding to an attack or incident, government sources, outside of some law enforcement liaison, will probably be less timely than commercial enterprises specializing in early warning and incident response measures. Attacks or exploits, however, are threats come to fruition. Initial government involvement in early warning and threat analysis would go a long way toward better prevention or deflection of these exploits.

*Q3b. What information have you been asked for by DHS that you feel uncomfortable providing? Why? What are the barriers to information sharing? Are changes in legislation or regulations needed to overcome these barriers?*

*A3b.* On numerous occasions, federal and State DHS authorities have asked us for information on our critical assets and on the protective measures (physical and cyber) surrounding them. Without the PCII program in place, we are very reluctant to provide that data, and have repeatedly declined their requests. We cannot be sure under the current situation of only partial implementation of the PCII program who will have access to that data. Once PCII is fully established and implemented, we will revisit information sharing and support the effort. We are committed to doing all we can to help the government protect our nation's critical infrastructure.

*Q4. Responding to Cyber Attacks*

*Q4a. If the information systems of a critical infrastructure company were attacked today, is the U.S. prepared to detect the attack and reel it or repair the systems quickly?*

*A4a.* While there are many companies that have successfully repelled one or more major cyber attacks, many more have not and a good number could not. Those that have the security technology and mature incident response programs are usually well equipped to handle both directed and general cyber attacks. Those that have few technical solutions in place or that have poorly defined incident response procedures are often victims of even the most well-known and preventable threats. So the answer to this question must be qualified with an "it depends on who is attacked" caveat. Overall as a country I believe we are not well equipped to repel such attacks.

*Q4b. What about if the attack were on the Internet?*

*A4b.* If attacks are recognized quickly (very likely) and there are preventive measures already in place and properly configured, responses after a major Internet attack can probably effectively thwart attackers. These measures range from network and system processes to equipment/communication redundancy.

*Q4c. What role can and should DHS and other public and private organizations play in these response activities?*

*A4c.* DHS should be providing the most up to date threat data available, along with analysis of potential and actual cyber threats. In addition, they should provide awareness information to companies that is substantive, citing examples of attacks, providing recommended solutions and adding real value to the knowledge base. To make this more meaningful, DHS might want to make this a collaborative effort with commercial companies that already have a large critical infrastructure customer base.

*Q4d. What are the barriers to DHS companies or other organizations providing a quick, effective and coordinated response?*

*A4d.* I can't speak for other companies, but regarding DHS, it needs to staff its ranks with true cyber security experts and be willing to pay the costs of their expertise. This does not mean hiring the standard group of government contractors. It means recruiting individuals from the commercial world that have industry credibility, can offer real knowledge and experience and feel that protecting critical infrastructure is a vital mission for our national security.

*Q4e. What is DHS doing to foster greater private sector efforts in cyber security, and what could the agency do that it is not doing now?*

*A4e.* DHS seems to be addressing most of the right areas as evidenced by the NIPP draft. They are also increasing involvement in industry groups, making sure their message is being effectively communicating. What they could add is accurate threat data and greater awareness of the impact that cyber attacks can have on the infrastructure and economy.

*Q4f. Are effective practices, procedures and technologies now available to guard against the adverse impacts of cyberspace vulnerabilities? Are there shortcomings for particular critical infrastructure areas?*

*A4f.* Currently there are effective practices, procedures and technologies available. And they will keep improving. The problem is that these are not used consistently across all infrastructure organizations. Unfortunately, with cyber security we're still only as strong as our weakest link.

## Answers to Post-Hearing Questions

*Responses by Andrew M. Geisse, Chief Information Officer, SBC Services, Inc.*

### Questions submitted by Chairman Sherwood L. Boehlert

*Q1. Measuring Cyber Security*

*How do you measure your company's cyber security? How do you determine if your company's level of cyber vulnerability is being reduced? How do you decide what is "secure enough"? Are there specific metrics you use in evaluating the cyber security of your company? How should the Department of Homeland Security (DHS) determine if the Nation is making progress? Are government mandates needed to increase the progress to get to "secure enough"?*

*A1.* There is no single metric or measurement that suffices to describe a company's cyber security readiness. SBC proactively determines the cyber security readiness of its environment through the use of internal and external audit reviews, secure system management compliance, application security compliance, routine scans to identify vulnerabilities, and periodic component review within the infrastructure. In addition, an annual assessment of deployed security solutions is conducted based upon new or changing requirements and conditions. SBC also has a team of IT Security professionals dedicated to the protection of its internal cyber resources. A key metric for SBC is the number of attempted and investigated intrusions within the environment and the corrective actions taken to address them.

As a way to measure private companies' progress towards cyber security, the Department of Homeland Security could use publicly reported information, such as annual Sarbanes-Oxley disclosure reports.

Government mandates should not be necessary. The DHS could focus on cyber security best practices and standards. Also helpful would be tools so companies could measure their compliance towards those best practices.

*Q2. Business Case for Cyber Security*

*Within your company, how do you make the business case for the costs associated with more secure information technology products? What can the Federal Government do to help you make this case and make investment in cyber security more attractive?*

*A2.* SBC well understands the need for cyber security, within the company infrastructure and as a service we can provide to users of our data products. Business cases to support cyber security preparedness to protect internal cyber resources must clearly define the risks to the business, the security tools needed and processes required, and then should be evaluated based on needs of the business. Most often, business cases supporting cyber security are developed because of new business opportunities, changing cyber technologies, new identified vulnerabilities, growth of our environment, or new legislative requirements.

Awareness of cyber security to the public can show a positive impact to businesses that help support cyber infrastructure (i.e., Internet). The more people understand virus protection, anti-spam tools, identity theft protection, and phishing risks, the better the Internet-connected community and services can perform on their behalf. Government education programs that could also be used within businesses would help defray internal education costs.

*Q3. Information Sharing*

*Q3a. What information would you find most helpful to receive from the government (especially DHS) or from other companies when you are making decisions related to what cyber security you need? When responding to an attack or incident?*

*A3a.* SBC would find it helpful if information from the DHS includes: current cyber vulnerabilities, attack methods, and attack sources. The most current information helps us prepare strategies to deal with new sources of attack and new methods of attack. The same can be said when responding to an incident. Understanding how an attack may occur and from where allows SBC to better prepare defenses that could block specific protocols or specific IP addresses.

*Q3b. What information have you been asked for by DHS that you feel uncomfortable providing? Why?*

*A3b.* Information that SBC has been asked to share that has made us uncomfortable includes items that we consider private within the company and restricted to only employees with a need to know. Examples include our private address spaces, server specifics (numbers, types, versions, and locations), vendors used and security infrastructure components. Typically, we are uncomfortable with sharing information that could be used to allow specific, targeted attacks against SBC. We also have an expectation from and an obligation to our customers to keep their information private and secure. Release of customer information to law enforcement should always follow the same strict protocol as any other subpoenaed information.

*Q3c. What are the principal barriers to information sharing? Are changes in legislation or regulations needed to overcome these barriers?*

*A3c.* It has been our experience that the principal barriers to information sharing between companies are; competition within an industry, potential negative public perception if cyber security intrusions occur, and the FOIA or other disclosure acts requiring federal agencies to disclose meeting proceedings or information provided.

*Q4. Responding to Cyber Attacks*

*If the information systems of a critical infrastructure company were attacked today, is the U.S. prepared to detect the attack and repel it or repair the systems quickly? What about if it were an attack on the Internet? What role can and should DHS and other public and private organizations play in these response activities? What are the barriers to DHS, companies, or other organizations providing a quick and effective and coordinated response?*

*A4.* I believe most large companies, especially those within the critical infrastructure, understand cyber security is a part of doing business within our Internet-connected world, today, and have taken precautionary measures to detect and protect against attacks.

The Internet itself is constantly attacked. The Internet, by definition, is a network of networks, and, as such, Internet service providers have an ability to segment portions of the network to prevent rampant abuse, if necessary.

Communications is the chief barrier to DHS' ability to coordinate a rapid and coordinated response to Internet problems. To provide a coordinated response, the DHS needs the ability to contact key Internet providers to focus on the immediate attack. This is not unlike the telecommunications requirement to have a National Security Emergency Preparedness (NSEP) organization which focuses on national telco events.

**Questions submitted by Representative Eddie Bernice Johnson**

*Q1. What is the Department of Homeland Security doing to foster greater private sector efforts in cyber security, and what could the agency do that it is not doing now?*

*A1.* SBC maintains close ties to government agencies responsible for national security. We work closely with them on a daily basis to receive and share security related information. The DHS is encouraged to continue to support the efforts of the following: the National Security Telecommunications Advisory Council (NSTAC), National Coordinating Center Telecom Information Sharing and Analysis Center (NCC Telecom ISAC), FBI's Infragard, and the National Security Information Exchange (NSIE).

DHS support of public awareness and education programs focused on cyber security would be a pro-active effort to help companies and the public be more aware of cyber security and the role they play to protect themselves.

*Q2. Are effective practices, procedures, and technologies now available to guard against the adverse impacts of cyberspace vulnerabilities? Are there shortcomings for particular critical infrastructure areas?*

*A2.* SBC utilizes security technologies and practices to guard against adverse cyber security vulnerabilities. We believe security tools and practices exist for industries to protect themselves. Our challenge is addressing new vulnerabilities as they appear. This requires technologies and processes to continuously react to the ever-changing environment. Consumers and industry must continue to hold vendors accountable and to focus their efforts on providing products and tools to meet cyber security best practices. Vendors need to recognize that cyber security is an administrative intensive effort and tools are needed to relieve this pressure.